Patchwork

& Quilting
with Kids

MAGGIE BALL

Published by

700 East State Street • Iola, WI 54990-0001
715-445-2214 • 888-457-2873
www.krause.com

To place an order or obtain a free catalog, please call 800-258-0929.

Library of Congress Catalog Number 2003108203
ISBN 0-87349-570-5

Photographer—Mark Frey, Yelm, Washington
Editor—Christine Townsend

The following trademarked or registered companies or product names appear in this book: Berol®, Coats and Clark®, ColorPlus Fabrics®, David Textiles®, Dream World™, Fabrico™, Fantastix™, Husqvarna Viking®, Mountain Mist®, Olfa®, Omnigrid®, Prym-Dritz®, Quilt Wizard™, Soft Touch®, Steam-a-Seam 2®, Sulky®, Ultimate Marking Pencil for Quilters™, Warm and Natural®, Ziploc®.

Dedication

To all beginning quilters—have fun!

Acknowledgments

I'd like to thank the many people who have contributed in a variety of ways to the creation of this book. Special thanks goes to all those mentioned below, whose support was crucial.

At Krause Publications, I was fortunate to work with Julie Stephani, acquisitions editor, and Christine Townsend, editor, whose patience and helpfulness ensured a smooth passage. Nancy Jewell, publicity director at Husqvarna Viking offered the loan of sewing machines for the kids. Terry Smith, the Northwest distributor, and my local dealers in Silverdale, Ray and Glenda Beardsley, made this possible. David Textiles, Inc., provided many yards of fabric for the projects, and gave me the opportunity to work with their creative director, Beth Bruske, to design fabric, some of which appears in the book. Several other companies, listed in the back of the book, contributed project tools and supplies.

It was a pleasure working with photographer Mark Frey. As always, he did a stellar job with the photography, and was unflustered by the photographic sessions with the kids when we wanted to achieve too much in a limited time. Vickie McKenney kindly allowed Mark and me to use space in her store, The Calico Basket, for all the studio photography. Wanda Rains quilted all but two of the commercially quilted quilts. The quality of her work and her readiness to jump in and help me at short notice, as well as her friendship, were much appreciated. When Wanda had back trouble and couldn't quilt, Carol Latham kindly bailed me out and quilted the two remaining quilts. Quilters' Anonymous preemie baby project coordinator, Karen Miltner, generously purchased, washed, and cut all the flannel backs for the kids to use for their baby blankets. Continuous support and good humor from my family was a tremendous prop. My husband, Nigel, solved my computing problems and helped me with formatting the text.

Hyla Middle School staff welcomed me and made their facilities available. Teacher, Chris Johnson, was a tower of strength and a wonderful partner. Her energy and enthusiasm for the projects with the kids was infectious and her contribution to this book enormous. The most important contributors are all the children whose wonderful works are featured. I enjoyed watching their creativity unfold in their fabric choices and patterns. They entered into the projects with gusto and were delightfully engaged, spending many hours of their free time quilting. I'd particularly like to mention my young quilting friend, Sophie Lowell, who at the age of 12 is in her third year of quilting with me. It has been my privilege to watch her develop into an accomplished quilter. She tackles each new project and technique with fresh ideas and excitement, and it is a joy to work with her. It is with much pleasure and gratitude that I share these kids' fine achievements with you in this book.

46 Section Two • Patchwork and Quilting Projects

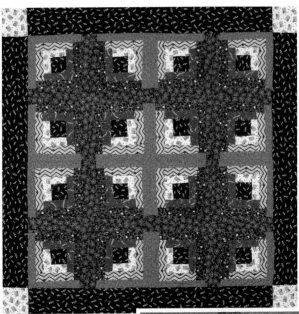

Introduction

This book is designed to introduce young and beginning quilters to machine piecing and quilting techniques through a series of small patchwork projects. It may be used by new quilters of any age, or as a teaching guide for seasoned quilters or teachers who would like to pass on their skills to the next generation. I hope that the wide variety of projects, including patchwork pillows, tote bags, wall hangings, little quilts, baby blankets, and lap quilts will provide you with appealing choices and creative options.

Quick gratification through the successful completion of a small project is a great way to encourage continuing interest. Once the piecing techniques have been mastered by making, for example, a patchwork pillow or a little quilt, lengthier projects become an exciting prospect. New quilters, especially children, are enthusiastic but may be overwhelmed by large projects that will take weeks or months to complete. They will be delighted to finish small projects while they learn the necessary skills to take on the bigger ones. Once they are confident with rotary cutting, sewing ¼" seam allowances, and basic piecing techniques, they will be ready to make a lap quilt.

Fabric choices and placement make each project unique, and kids and adults alike will enjoy selecting their favorite colors and patterns. Some patterns in the book are repeated in a variety of ways to demonstrate what a difference color, orientation of the quilt block, and the block settings can make. I encourage you to experiment and make your own patterns. Blank pattern sheets are provided for you to copy, color in, cut up, and rearrange. Multiple paper blocks can be assembled into posters. This is a great way to introduce kids to the mathematics of quilting, while allowing them to be creative. Part of the fun of quilting is making the design your own, and I hope that you will enjoy exploring some of the many possibilities.

Maggie and Chris plan the projects.

Hyla Middle School teacher, Chris Johnson, and I were fortunate to spend many quilting sessions with her students (ages 11 to 14). Chris ran a series of quilting electives that met twice a week for six weeks. In the twelve 45-minute sessions, the kids became proficient at using the cutting tools and sewing machines. They made pre-emie baby blankets to donate to the Neonatal Intensive Care Unit at the University of Washington Hospital, and patchwork pillows for themselves. We also organized a community service-oriented quilt club after school once a week, open to anyone, whether or not they signed up for the elective. Projects included making more baby blankets and working on Star blocks for a school auction quilt.

The Hyla children, who are featured in this book, astounded me by their eagerness to design their own blocks and quilt patterns. They used the patterns I provided and improvised, drawing out the layout in their journals. Sometimes these evolved as the project progressed; for example, small pieced sections could be oriented in a variety of ways, or a large square cut too small by mistake could be replaced by a 4-patch. The enthusiasm with which the kids embraced the challenges, and their desire to make their very own designs, were a joy to behold. In fact, they were much more prepared to experiment and play with the patchwork than most of the beginning adult quilters I have taught. Such creativity is to be encouraged. Children will become totally absorbed in their projects and, provided there is enough time, they can be free to try some of the many variations on the basic patterns *and* have great fun.

I hope that you will be inspired by the achievements of the kids featured in this book, enjoy the projects, and have fun creating your own unique quilts.

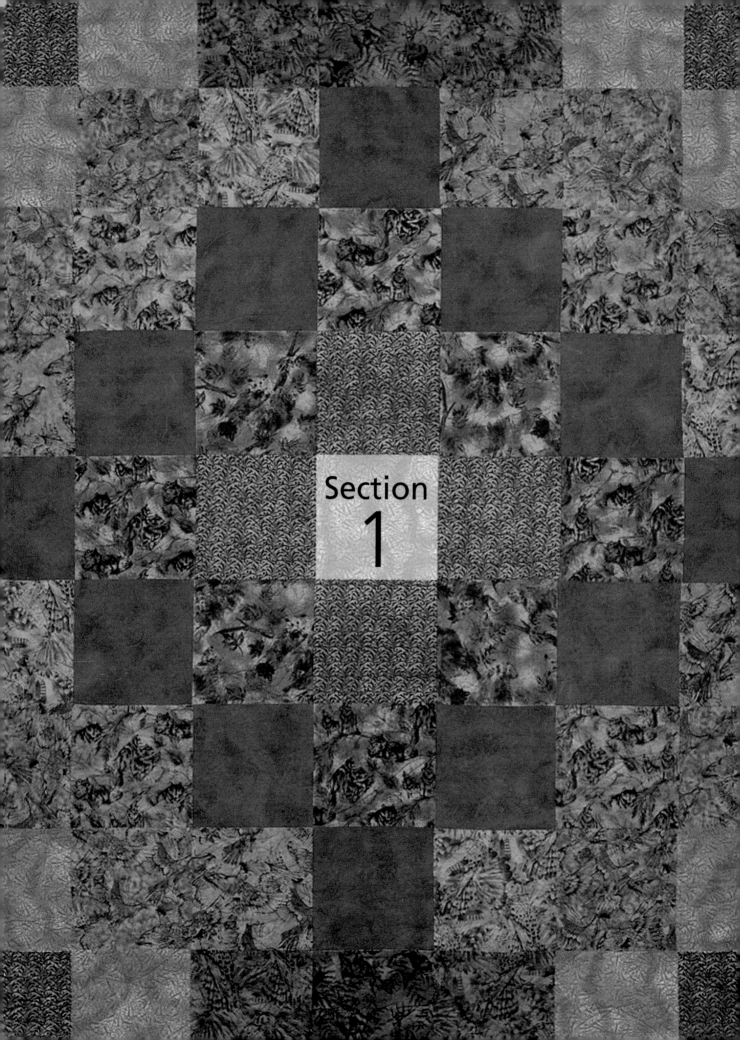

Section
1

Quilts are composed of three layers: A patchwork or whole cloth top, a batting middle, and a back. The quilt sandwich is held together with quilting stitches. The quilting stitches are a vital component and are not only functional, but can also significantly enhance the design of the quilt.

The quilt top may be pieced in an enormous variety of patterns and designs. The possibilities are endless. Even if you take a traditional block or pattern, you can make your own choices of color and fabric placement so that your creation is unique. It is fun to experiment with different fabrics. You will soon discover how dramatically a pattern can change depending on the color and value placement of the patchwork pieces. I find this exciting and challenging. Every quilt is different and provides a new set of opportunities. All well-seasoned quilters have a fabric stash, and they are always on the lookout for more fabric to add to their collection. If you catch the quilting bug, you too will soon gather a pile of fabrics for potential projects!

There are many different techniques for making quilts. This section introduces you to the tools we use for quilting and variety of basic timesaving methods for machine piecing patchwork. Once you have mastered the basics and completed a small project, you should feel confident to attempt something larger and more complex.

Patchwork and Quilting **B•A•S•I•C•S**

Pieced quilts are made by cutting fabric into pieces and joining the pieces together. The pieces can be any geometric shape, as long as they will fit together. Many quilts are composed of quilt blocks. These are usually square and may be pieced or appliquéd. A 4-patch is a pieced block divided into four equal parts; a 9-patch is one divided into nine equal parts;and one divided into 16 equal parts, is a 16-patch. These parts may be further subdivided into smaller squares, rectangles, and triangles. Quilt block patterns are often repeated in the quilt, or two different blocks may be alternated. You can arrange the blocks however you like, and add sashing strips to separate them and borders around the outside. A quilt in which every block is different is called a sampler.

In appliqué quilts, the pieces are cut and applied to larger background pieces of fabric. Traditionally, the seam allowance of the appliqué piece is needleturned under as the piece is sewn by hand. There are several different ways to appliqué. The appliqué projects in this book are fusible appliquéd, in which the pieces are heat bonded with an adhesive webbing onto the background.

Project Preparation, Tools and Supplies

Here is a list of useful quilting supplies. These are not all required, so if you are just beginning, don't feel overwhelmed. You can gradually acquire items as you need them. The most time-saving tools, after the sewing machine, are the **rotary cutter,** used with **a cutting mat**, and a 6" x 24" **quilters' ruler**. Note: Make sure the blade is closed when the rotary cutter is not in your hand. *Rotary cutters are very sharp and are off limits for children without strict supervision.*

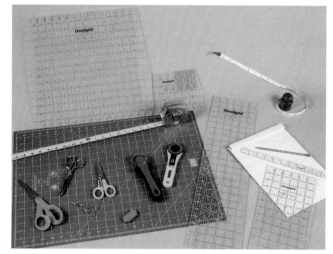

Measuring and cutting tools.

useful supplies

Sewing machine
Iron and ironing board
Rotary cutter, 45mm
Cutting mat, minimum size
　17" x 23"
Quilters' ruler, 6" x 24"
15" x 15" square ruler
12" ruler
Sewing scissors
Paper cutting scissors

Graph paper
Small sticky labels
Locking plastic bags for storage
Mechanical pencil with fine lead
　(0.5mm)
Variety of 100 percent cotton
　fabrics (flannel optional)
Freezer paper
Fusible webbing
Batting

Needles and pins
Thread
Decorative threads
Old dessert spoon
Marking pencils or chalk pencils
T-pins for basting
Safety pins
Seam ripper
Masking tape
Quilt wall

A quilt wall (highly recommended) is an area of a wall covered with batting or flannel where you can arrange patchwork pieces and blocks, and stand back to view them. The fabric will cling to the wall but can be peeled off easily and rearranged into the desired configuration. The backside of a vinyl table cloth makes a convenient temporary quilt wall. It can even be folded up and the fabric pieces will remain in place.

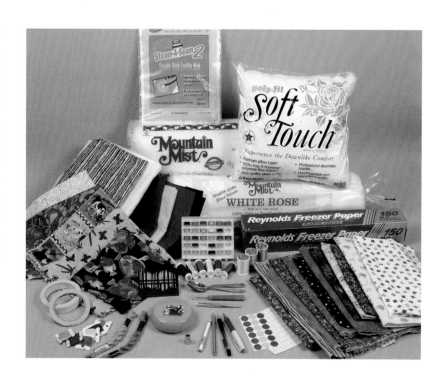

Project supplies and notions.

Choosing Fabrics for Your Projects

Quilters usually use 100 percent cotton fabrics. You will be delighted by the choice of fabrics available. Recently, there has been a huge increase in the number of printed flannels. Flannel makes wonderfully soft, warm quilts, but it is a little bulkier to work with than regular cotton. I've used it for a couple of projects in this book, ones in which the pieces are large.

I recommend pre-washing all your fabrics before you start sewing. This will take care of any shrinkage and remove the fabric sizing. You can also make sure that the fabrics are colorfast and do not bleed. This is rarely a problem if you avoid the poor quality fabrics.

Choose fabrics that you like and will make your patchwork patterns show up. Your choice will personalize your quilt and make it unique. If you don't know where to begin, try choosing a multi-colored print, (which could be a theme print), then pick out the matching colors. Sometimes it isn't easy to visualize your finished quilt, and it may not turn out exactly as expected. You don't have to make all your choices before you start. Often, I make my quilt blocks or the center of a quilt before I decide which fabrics to use in the sashing strips and borders. Once the blocks are completed, I put them on my quilt wall and audition different fabrics to see which ones I like the best. You can take your blocks to the fabric store and lay them out with a variety of fabrics. There will be no shortage of people around to offer their opinions and help you, but ultimately, the choice is yours. If you take young quilters shopping, let them make their own choices. If they need to adjust their choice to include a wider range of values, simply make suggestions to provide more options from which they can choose. They will want to make their own decisions and will be excited about working with the fabric that they have picked out. Color, value, and print scale are all important factors to consider; the most successful quilts are often the ones with the most variety.

Color

Color is usually the first thing we notice about a quilt, and if the color combination is appealing, we are immediately drawn into looking at everything else. Kids tend to have a strong sense of what colors they like, and are often more decisive than adults who have preconceived ideas about what colors they think should go together. After more than ten years of quilting, I discovered that the color wheel theory really works!

The primary colors—yellow, red, and blue—are pure colors that cannot be made by mixing. They are the basis for all other colors. The secondary colors—orange, purple, and green—are made by mixing equal parts of two primary colors. The three secondary colors lie halfway between the three primary colors on the color wheel. Mixing equal parts of a primary color and its closest secondary color makes tertiary, or intermediate, colors.

Black and white are not included in the color wheel. Black is an absence of color, and white is made up of all the other colors. Tints are colors with white added, tones are colors with gray added, and shades are colors with black added.

Primary Colors

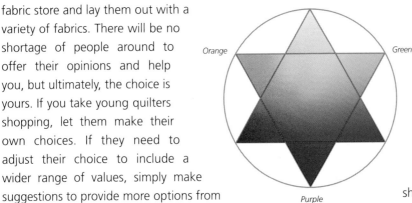

Yellow

Red　　　　*Blue*

Secondary Colors

Orange　　　　*Green*

Purple

Recommended Color Schemes

Complementary

Color combinations of colors directly opposite each other on the color wheel (for example, red and green, purple and yellow, blue and orange).

Split Complementary

One color in combination with a color on each side of its complement (for example, yellow with blue-purple and red-purple).

Triad

Three colors equally spaced on the color wheel (for example, the primary colors).

Tetrad

Contrast of four or more colors from all around the color wheel (for example, orange, red, blue, and green).

Feel free to add black and/or white to any of your color combinations. Black will intensify the colors and make them stronger, and white will dilute or soften them.

Color Schemes That Are *Not* Recommended (except with the addition of black or white)

Monochromatic

Any shade, tint, or tone of one color only.

Analogous

Adjacent colors within a 90 degree segment of the color wheel (for example, yellow-green, green, and blue-green).

Warning! A little bit of yellow goes a long way. Yellow is a powerful color that draws the eye and tends to dominate. Remember that people vary in their perception of color and in their likes and dislikes. Colors change in appearance when they are adjacent to other colors. They also change according to the level of light—you know that just from looking out of the window at different times of day or by comparing the view on

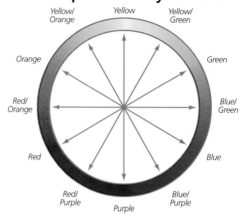

Complementary Colors

sunny and cloudy days. The most important thing is to select colors that you like, and then you will enjoy working on your quilt. Be prepared to experiment and have fun trying out different color combinations.

Value

Value is the lightness or darkness of a color. Using a variety of values to create contrast is very important.

Select a variety of fabrics—dark, medium, and light—in value. If you have trouble distinguishing the values, take your fabrics to a black-and-white copy machine. The black-and-white image will show you the lightness and darkness, and you will be able to see the amount of

Fabrics of a variety of values.

contrast. Some colors, such as yellow or fluorescent colors, may read paler than you might expect, and other colors, such as blue or red, may be darker. There is a tendency to use too many fabrics in the medium value range. Even if the colors are different, if the values are too similar in a quilt block and lack contrast, the pattern of the block will be indistinct.

Value is just as vital as color and will define the artistic composition of the quilt.

Print Scale

The size of the print on the fabric is another important characteristic. Again, variety is best. Solid colors have no printed pattern, but can be used in combination with prints. Some fabrics appear as solids from a distance, but have subtle variations in color or a very small pattern. Look at the pattern size and also the density. The pattern may be sparse, dense, or anything in between. Large-scale prints sometimes have big areas of the background between the printed patterns. Try to imagine how they will look when they are cut up into small pieces for patchwork. Maybe they would be better suited to quilt backs or wide borders.

As you can see from the 9-patch blocks shown below, the pattern disappears in the one using all large-scale prints, even though there is variation in the value.

Be wary of stripes and directional prints, which require very accurate cutting and piecing. Stripes which run perpendicular on long strips are fine and can add pizzazz to the quilt, but stripes that need to be aligned parallel can be awkward. Sometimes the pattern is not printed parallel to the grain of the fabric and this can cause additional problems. You may decide to use a particular motif or section of fabric for a piece in your quilt. You can selectively cut it out—this is called fussy-cutting.

In summary, color, value, and scale are all important factors to consider when selecting fabric. Your choice will be unique and reflect your taste and personality. If you don't like the choices you made, try some different combinations—there's plenty more fabric out there. You will quickly learn what works and what doesn't. Don't take it too seriously … you are supposed to be having fun!

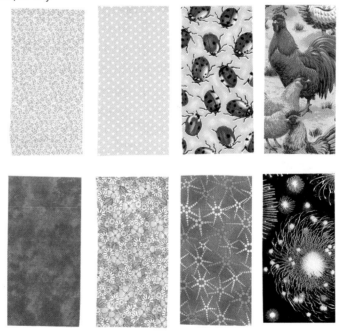

9-patch blocks made from similar and contrasting values.

Selection of fabrics shows a range of print size.

9-patch blocks made from different print sizes.

Fabric Basics

When cutting fabric, you need to pay attention to the direction of the grain—that is, the way in which the fabric is woven.

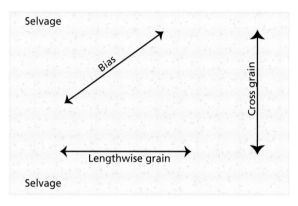

The term "straight of grain" refers to either the lengthwise or cross grains. Bias edges stretch and easily become misshapen, so patchwork pieces are usually cut with as many sides as possible aligned with the straight grain. Quilters always try to ensure that the outer edges of quilt blocks are on the straight grain to reduce distortion. Strips, squares, and rectangles should always be cut in alignment with the grain unless they are being fussy-cut for a particular motif in the fabric. Obviously, right-angled triangles have to have at least one bias edge. If the long side of the triangle has to be on the outer edge of the block, the triangle will have two bias edges.

On some fabrics, especially solid colored fabrics, it is hard to tell the right side from the back. If you can't tell, then don't worry about it! There is no reason why you shouldn't use the back of a fabric as the "right" side if you want.

When piecing patchwork, a ¼" seam allowance is used. Always cut your fabric pieces large enough to include this ¼" on each side. For example, a 3" square should be cut 3½" square to allow for the ¼" on each side, and a 4" x 6" rectangle should be cut 4½" x 6½".

The **finished size** is the measurements of a completed piece, block, or quilt top without the seam allowances. When we refer to 9" or 12" quilt blocks, this is the finished size. The **unfinished size** is the measurements of a completed piece, block, or quilt top before it is joined to other bits of fabric. The unfinished size includes the seam allowance. The unfinished sizes of 9" and 12" blocks are 9½" and 12½", respectively.

Planning Your Project

Spend a little time planning, being realistic about the size of the project you want to tackle and your skill level. Setting a goal for completion is often helpful but shouldn't cause stress! Making notes will help you to stay organized and save time. Draw a sketch with annotations so that you know the positions of the different fabrics. Record the sizes of the pieces to be cut (don't forget to include the ¼" seam allowances) and the number of pieces needed of each fabric. You can refer to this anytime and see exactly what should be done next. Without this record, it is easy to lose track of your patchwork pieces, especially if you do not have time to cut all of them in one sitting. The projects in this book have supply lists, but if you modify them in any way, you may have to recalculate your fabric requirements.

The children at Hyla Middle School each had a pizza box for storage of their fabric, patchwork pieces, and journal (large zip lock bags also work for small projects). They made journals from ¼" squared graph paper so it was easy for them to draw diagrams of their patchwork patterns and keep notes.

Estimating Yardage

All of the projects include supply lists, but you may need to calculate fabric yardage for quilts of your own design, or lap quilts in which you improvise on the pattern provided. A little simple math on paper should take care of it relatively easily. Remembering that the fabric is 42" wide, work out how many pieces of the size you want will fit across one width of fabric. Allow yourself some extra fabric in case of errors. The shelf life of individual fabrics is relatively short and it isn't always easy to find the same fabric when you go back to the store.

Let's take the Snowball lap quilt as an example (see page 112). This quilt is composed of 25 pictorial blocks alternating with 24 light blocks. Twenty-four 7½" light squares are needed; 42 divided by 7½ is 5 with a little left over, so you can cut five squares from one width of fabric. You need 24 squares, so cut five full-width 7½" strips; (5 x 7½) equals 37½" of fabric—so buy 1¼ yards. For the corner triangles, (100) 2¾" squares are needed for the pictorial blocks, and (96) 2¾" squares are needed for the light blocks. Forty-two divided by

2¾ is 15 with a little left over, so you can cut 15 squares from one width of fabric. To cut 96 or 100, you will need 7 (100 divided by 15 rounded up to next whole number) full-width 2¾" strips, which is 19¼"—so buy ⅔ yard of each fabric.

Borders require long strips of fabric unless you plan to piece them (see the section on borders, page 30). Quilt backs will need two full lengths of fabric if they are wider than 42", or they can be pieced from several fabrics (see the section on quilt backs, page 31).

To calculate the amount of fabric needed for binding, measure the perimeter of the quilt and work out how many full-width 2½" strips to cut. For example, the Snowball lap quilt is 59" x 59", with a perimeter of 236". Six 2½" strips (236 divided by 40 and rounded up to the nearest whole number) are needed, which is 15" of fabric, so allow ½ a yard. If you have trouble making estimates, quilt store staff should be able to assist. Don't be afraid to ask for help if you need it.

Rotary Cutting Fabric

Rotary cutters are wonderful, timesaving cutting tools. Accurately-sized pieces of fabric may be cut quickly in multiple layers. I recommend 45mm rotary cutters, mats at least 17" x 23", and Omnigrid rulers (6" x 24", and 15" square). The 15" square is not essential, but is extremely useful for cutting blocks larger than 6" square. If you are unfamiliar with these tools, seek the help of another quilter or ask at your local quilt store for a demonstration.

You must **never allow the rotary cutter to leave your hand with the blade exposed**. I cannot emphasize this enough. Always retract the blade, even if you are going to immediately pick up the cutter again to make another cut (who knows, you may be interrupted). Make a habit of closing the blade before you put it down. I'm very strict about this when I am teaching, and am constantly checking and reminding my students—even well-seasoned quilters who should know better!

Follow these: steps to accurately cut your fabric.

1. Press the fabric.
2. Fold the fabric selvage to selvage. You may find that the raw edge has not been cut straight, but make the fold so that the fabric will lie flat.
3. Fold the fabric again in the same direction, and place it flat on the cutting mat with the selvage edges at the top. You now have four layers of fabric.

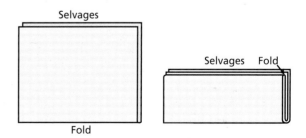

4. Cut to straighten the raw edge. Line up a horizontal line on your 6" x 24" ruler with the fold at the bottom of the fabric. Move the ruler as close as possible to the raw edge of the fabric so there is a minimum of waste, but so that the raw edges on all the

layers of fabric are exposed. Hold the ruler firmly in position with one hand, keeping fingers and thumb at least 1" away from the cutting edge. Hold the cutter as you would a sharp knife with your forefinger extended, and the shaft upright with the blade flush against the ruler. Apply some downward pressure and make the cut in one motion away from yourself, keeping the blade next to the edge of the ruler. Maintaining the position of the ruler, remove the raw edge that you just cut. If your cut did not penetrate all the layers, repeat the cut with your ruler still in place. Now you have a straight edge!

5. To make the next cut, carefully rotate the fabric without disturbing the straight edge, or move around the table to the other side of the cutting board. Cut strips the desired width, using the ruler or square. If your original cut was not straight, or the ruler slipped on the second cut, you will have doglegs in the strip. Straighten the edge and try again!

6. Counter-cut strips to make blocks or pieces of the desired size.

7. Don't forget to close the blade on the rotary cutter. The blade is very sharp!

To cut strips or squares larger than 6", use a square ruler. A variety of ruler sizes is available. My favorite is the 15" square. If you do not have a square ruler, you can use the grid on the cutting mat. Don't forget to cut your pieces large enough to include the ¼" seam allowance on each side.

Taking the time to use rulers carefully and cut precisely is time well spent. Your cuts should be clean. If there are any irregular edges, straighten them up before cutting your next strip or patchwork piece. Sometimes, when you make multiple counter-cuts on strips, the edge gradually becomes slightly skewed. Simply square it off after every four or five cuts, or as soon as you see that it is out of alignment. Accurate cutting is very important and will make all the difference to the ease with which your patchwork pieces fit together.

ABOVE: Ryan straightening up the raw edge.

RIGHT: Sarah cutting strips for her blanket border.

Sewing Machines and Extras

There are many different sewing machines on the market. You do not need a fancy machine to make a quilt, but you do need one that is in good working order. All patchwork piecing is sewn with a simple straight stitch with a ¼" seam allowance. In some of the projects, backstitches are occasionally used. Zigzag or serpentine stitches are useful for top stitching and quilting.

If you want to machine quilt your work, you will need a dual-feed walking foot for your machine for straight-line quilting. The walking foot has moving parts that help to feed the top layer of the quilt sandwich through the machine at the same rate as the bottom layer. If a regular presser foot is used, the pressure on the three layers is too great, and the top puckers. For free-motion quilting, you will need a darning or embroidery foot and the ability to drop or cover the feed dogs on the machine.

Projects involving fused appliqué hearts use a variety of machine embroidery stitches. The more complicated the machine, the more elaborate you can get with embroidery stitches.

For example, lettering may be added and fancier stitch patterns. Children are used to using computers and are not intimidated by computerized sewing machines. In fact, they think the machines are really cool, and of course, they are right! My 12-year-old quilting buddy, Sophie, uses my Viking Designer I machine and loves it; so do I.

The extension table is an added luxury, which makes piecing and quilting easier, especially when the quilt grows.

At Hyla Middle School, we used Viking Daisy 325 and Viking Freesia 425 machines, kindly loaned to us by the company. The Daisy 325 is a mechanical machine with all the basic stitches, and the Freesia is computerized and more complicated with over 20 different stitches, including a variety of embroidery stitches. The machines were easy for the children to use and reliable. Viking machines even

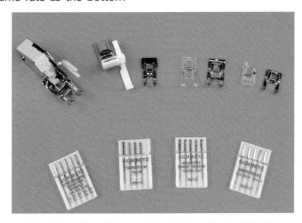

Machine feet and needles. Feet from left to right: Dual feed foot (walking foot) for machine quilting; Quilt Wizard and ¼" feet for making ¼" seam allowances; Plastic and metal regular utility feet; Darning/embroidery foot for free motion machine quilting; Open-toed appliqué foot for decorative stitches on fused appliqué.

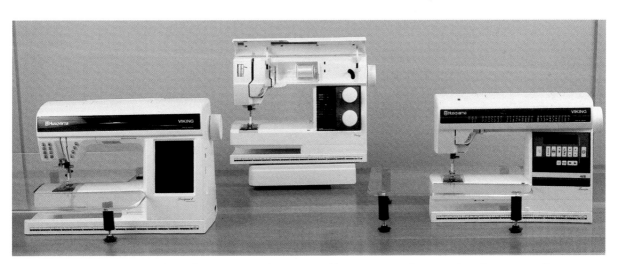

Sewing machines, left to right: Designer I with extension table, Daisy 325, and Freesia 425 with extension table.

have arrows showing the thread pathway for threading. Another nice feature is the lack of a bobbin case. The bobbin simply drops straight into the machine.

For machine piecing, use Size 80 needles, either Sharps or Universal (Sharps have sharper points). The Size 80s should serve most of your needs, but for machine embroidery with metallic threads, use the Size 90 Topstitch needle. Quilting needles may be used for machine quilting. Needles will become dull and should be changed after every five to eight hours of use.

For all patchwork piecing, a standard ¼" seam allowance is used. For most machines, a ¼" presser foot is available. Simply line up the raw edges of the fabric with the edge of the foot as you sew to make a perfect ¼" seam. For the Viking Designer I, the ¼" foot is not needed because the needle position may be moved to a ¼" setting. Kids age 11 and up usually have no problem with the ¼" foot, and after a little practice, they are proficient at sewing accurately. Younger children may benefit from a little extra help. The Quilt Wizard is a special foot attachment with a plastic protrusion. The raw edges of fabric are butted up against the plastic part and it is much easier than constantly keeping an eye on the edge of the presser foot. I worked with Harry, age seven, who made a patchwork pillow. He had trouble with the ¼" presser foot, so we tried the Quilt Wizard and it was perfect for him. If anything, err toward a scant ¼" but never toward a generous ¼".

If you do not have a ¼" presser foot or attachment, you may place a piece of masking tape or moleskin on the throat plate. Use ¼" ruled graph paper to determine the exact position to place the tape. Trim the edge of the piece of graph paper along one of the marked lines, then the stitching line can be sewn a measured distance from the edge of the paper (the seam allowance). When the needle is positioned exactly ¼" from the edge of the paper, place the masking tape next to the edge of the paper. Remove the paper and sew a seam on fabric, keeping the raw edges of the fabric next to the edge of the masking tape. Check your accuracy, and adjust the tape if necessary.

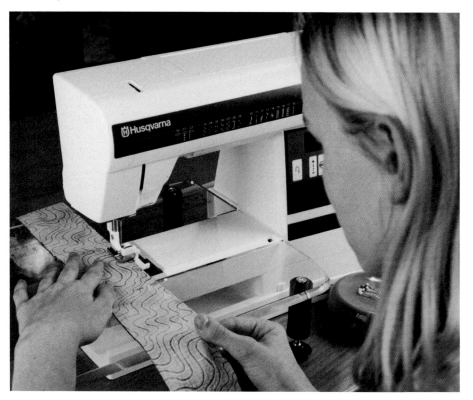

Alicen uses the Quilt Wizard attachment to make a ¼" seam.

Using the Sewing Machine

Children 11 years or older usually have the motor skills and level of maturity necessary to use a sewing machine. Of course, this is not a hard and fast rule. There are some extremely capable nine-year-olds and some very uncoordinated 15-year-olds. Younger children can sew too, with the one-on-one help of an adult. Children may be apprehensive about using a sewing machine, but their initial hesitation is soon dispelled when they sit down and see that it is not difficult to operate, and it sews neatly and quickly.

Make sure that the sewing machine is in good working order. If you can adjust the speed of the motor on the machine, slow it down, so that you have a little more control until you get used to it. Alternatively, the foot pedal may be doctored with a wedge of cardboard, so that it cannot be depressed all the way. Usually this is not necessary, since good control comes after only a short period of practicing. Adjust the height of the seat so that you are comfortable. Young children may need a box or a couple of telephone directories to raise the foot pedal to within easy reach.

Make friends with your machine and become familiar with the way it operates. If you have never used a machine before, start by sewing on a piece of graph paper along the lines with no thread. The needle will punch holes in the paper so you can see whether you are sewing in a straight line, and you will become familiar with the feel of the motor.

Megan uses a ¼" foot to sew two strips.

And now for sewing on fabric! Make 4-patches using scrap fabric strips (cut when practicing to use the rotary cutter), to practice making a consistent ¼" seam allowance.

For those new to machine sewing, there is a tendency to want to pull the fabric through the machine. The feed dogs on the machine do this for you, and they do not need any help. Both hands should be positioned in front of the presser foot and be used to gently guide the fabric as it moves toward the needle.

When you finish sewing and want to remove the fabric from the machine, raise the presser foot and gently pull the piece away to cut the threads. If there is any resistance and the threads do not move easily, manually adjust the position of the needle until the threads pull away smoothly.

Kate practices sewing on graph paper.

Teaching Tips

If you are teaching children a small project, such as the patchwork pillows, and they have never used sewing machines before, I suggest no more than four children per teacher/adult helper. If you have four children and can provide at least two sewing machines in good working order, you will save a great deal of time. The children can share the machines, and while you are helping one child with cutting, the others can be practicing on the machines. If they bring their own machines, valuable time will be wasted setting up the machines. Parents will often give their children an old machine that has been sitting in a closet for years and they don't even know whether it works. If reliable machines are set up and ready to go when the kids arrive for the class, frustration levels and waiting time for individual attention will be reduced enormously.

For longer projects, where the kids come for several sessions, you will have time to teach them more about threading the machines and the mechanics. They can bring their own machines, but only if it is clear that you expect their machines to be in good working order. Children respond differently according to their age, skill level, and temperament. Young children require much more help with the machines than teenagers. Teach them to respect the machine and treat it kindly—no slamming down the presser foot or racing the motor. Be prepared to be patient and usually the children will be patient about waiting for help too. It's intense, but great fun and the children's enthusiasm will delight you!

Chris helps Megan and Layne.

Machine Embroidery

Machine embroidery is fun to add as embellishment to patchwork. There are a variety of machine stitches you can use, depending on your sewing machine. You can adjust each stitch by changing the stitch length and width to create a different look and more choices. I made some samples using the Viking Freesia 425 machine to illustrate the variations and to experiment with different types of threads. The shiny and variegated threads are fun to use and Sulky has a great selection.

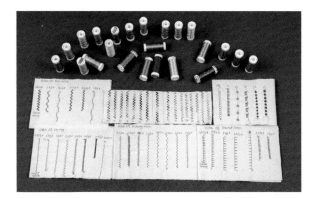

Embroidery stitch samples with a variety of decorative threads.

Fused appliqué provides a stable substrate for the embroidery and there is no need to use a tear away stabilizer on the back. Use Steam-a-Seam 2 to fuse hearts and hands for a variety of projects. Follow the instructions for fusible appliqué found on page 43. You can blanket stitch or zigzag around the outside of the shape, and then add more decorative stitches across the heart. An open-toed appliqué foot is the preferred foot, but is not essential. A regular foot will work, provided it has enough space for the needle to move sideways for the decorative stitches. If in doubt, consult your machine manual.

If your machine will make letters, you can embroider writing onto your patchwork (see Uncle Sam's pillow, page 60, and Sophie's lap quilt, page 108). Put tear-away stabilizer on the backside of the fabric in the area to be embroidered so that the fabric will stay flat and free of puckers. Pull the thread ends to the backside and tie them off to prevent the stitching from coming out. If you use 40 wt. threads, you should not need to adjust the upper tension on the machine. For metallic threads change the needle to a Size 90 Topstitch and reduce the upper tension slightly.

Machine Piecing the Patchwork

When sewing patchwork pieces, always use a consistent ¼" seam allowance unless instructed otherwise. See the previous section for instructions and help to sew with a precise ¼" seam allowance. In general, we do not backstitch when sewing patchwork pieces together, but it is important to sew from the very beginning to the end of the seam (starting ¹⁄₁₆"

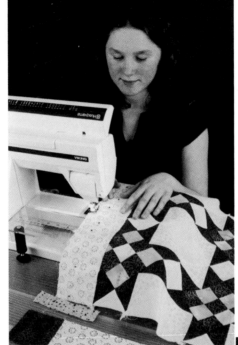

or ⅛" from beginning is not good enough). All the pieces are joined onto other pieces, but those two or three stitches between the edge of the fabric and the next seam are vital. If the stitching line doesn't start right at the edge and finish right at the edge, it is far more likely to come apart beyond ¼" and you will have holes. To sew from the very edge of the fabric without the thread tangling up, use a spacer strip and assembly line piece as instructed on page 23.

Megan sews a border strip onto her blanket.

Reduce your stitch size. Most sewing machines are set up for dressmaking and on a scale of 1-4; the automatic setting for straight stitching is around 2.5. Turn it down a tad to 2.0 or just above 2.0. This will also reduce the chance of stitches at the beginnings and ends of seams coming apart. If you are sewing with flannel, increase the stitch size to just below 3.0 and if possible, reduce the pressure of the presser foot. Flannel is soft and much more stretchy than regular cotton. You will notice that the top piece of flannel tends to stretch and easily pucker as you sew, especially if it is a bias edge. Reducing the presser foot pressure and using a larger stitch size eases these problems, and frequent pinning will also help. I suggest using flannel only for those projects that have large pieces, such as pillowcases, the Ohio Star, and 81-patch lap quilts.

Accuracy and consistency in cutting and sewing are very important for all your patchwork pieces to fit together perfectly.

Pinning

Before you sew, put the right sides of the fabric together and pin them along the edge to be sewn. Place the pins perpendicular to the sewing line with the heads extending ¼" to ½" beyond the edge on the right hand side so that they may be easily removed with the right hand when you are sewing on the machine. Left-handed people may like to pin with the pinheads on the left side, so that they can remove the pins easily with their left hand as they sew.

You may sew over the pins, but go slowly and make sure that the pins are perpendicular to the sewing line. If the pins are skewed, or if you sew too fast, you may break your sewing machine needle and/or bend the pin. I only sew over pins when I am sewing across a seam intersection, for example, at the center of a 4-patch, or at

Keri pins strips of squares.

Megan pins the left-handed way.

cal pin stabilizes the position of the triangle points. Remove the vertical pin before you sew.

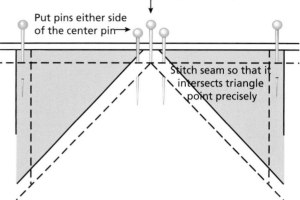

Stick pin straight down through triangle point.
Remove after the other two pins are in place.

Put pins either side
of the center pin→

Stitch seam so that it intersects triangle point precisely

triangle points. As you become more proficient at sewing accurately and keeping the raw edges of the fabric together, you will use fewer pins and may be able to sew strips together without using pins at all. Always use pins for seam intersections, when sewing bias edges together, and for adding border strips.

Katie sews over the pins.

When joining units composed of triangles, take extra care so that the seam allowance does not swallow up a point and blunt a triangle. You don't want the triangle points floating on the background either. The piecing should be precise so that the triangle points are intact and exactly next to the seam line. This can be tricky, especially where several triangle points come together, such as in the middle of a pinwheel. Accurate pinning before you sew will help enormously. The area around the triangle points is usually thick from the seam allowances and difficult to pin. When you try to pin through the extra bulk you may find that the triangle points are no longer exactly aligned. A solution to this problem is to match up the triangle points exactly and stick a pin straight down through them. Then add a pin on either side, very close to the vertical pin. The pins you add can be pushed through the seam allowances at an angle as long as the verti-

If your cutting or piecing is inaccurate and you are unable to correct it, sometimes you will need to ease in extra amounts of fabric when you join two pieces. Pin so that the excess is distributed evenly along the length of the seam. Do this by pinning the ends and centers together first, then halfway between the center and the end, and so on. If the longer of the fabrics is placed on the underside when you machine sew, it will be easier to accommodate the excess. If you are dealing with two pieced sections, pin all the seam intersections first to make sure they are in the correct position and then, if necessary, add more pins in between, rather than just starting at one end and pinning without paying attention to the piecing pattern.

Pressing

Use the iron on the hot cotton setting (unless you are sewing with material that isn't cotton), preferably with steam. Young children will need strict supervision, but they quickly grasp the concept of hot! In general, seam allowances are pressed to one side, and if possible, toward the darkest fabric. After sewing the seam, set it by pressing along the stitching line, then open it and press from the right side, using the edge of the

Layne presses to set the seam; and presses from the right side.

each piece as you feed it through the machine.

Cut the thread between the pieces in the assembly line chain to separate them before you press the seams.

Sewing Squares

An ideal first patchwork project for beginners is to sew squares together. You can make Simple 4-patches or 9-patches into pillows, add them to tote bags, or arrange 25 squares to make a little quilt or receiving blanket. Squares are always pieced in rows and then the rows are joined. Always plan the order of the sewing so that each seam is a straight line with no insetting and backstitching required. If you always begin by sewing your

iron, not the point, along the seam line to make sure that there are no folds and that the pieces lie flat.

In some cases, where several seam allowances come together, seams may be pressed open rather than to one side, such as on the final seam of a pinwheel where eight triangle points and seam allowances come together in the center. Further pressing instructions are provided with the piecing instructions.

patchwork shapes into square units, then you can easily join them together in rows in this way.

To make a single 4-patch or 9-patch, pin and join the squares into rows. I find it useful to arrange the pieces

Assembly Line Piecing

To assembly line or chain sew, start by sewing on a small scrap of fabric folded in half. I call this the **spacer strip**. Sew to the edge of the spacer strip, and then feed your patchwork pieces through the machine one after another. When you finish each batch of sewing, feed in the spacer strip. This saves time and thread, and enables you to start stitching at the very edge of the fabric without the thread knotting or the fabric gathering. If you make a habit of feeding in the spacer strip every time you complete each batch of sewing, you will always be ready to start sewing again. Be careful not to overlap the pieces as you feed them in, otherwise they will be sewn together! The thread will not tangle if you sew a couple of stitches between

Keri assembly line pieces strips of squares, starting with a spacer strip.

Hollie and Valerie piece squares for a 25-patch.

on a sheet of paper, and then I can see which ones to join. For the 9-patch, pin and join the first two squares in each row, and then add the third squares to the rows. Press the seams toward the dark fabric. When you join the rows, the seams will butt together nicely and the seam allowances will be pressed in opposite directions. Always pin at the seam intersections to make sure they are accurately positioned when you sew.

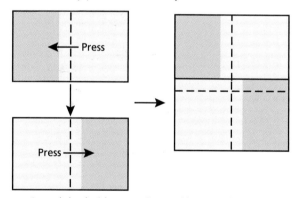

4-patch back side—pressing and butting the seams.

Griffen arranges his squares on the quilt wall.

If you are making multiple 4-patches or 9-patches, use the strip piecing method.

When you sew large numbers of squares together, sew them together into rows. For a 25-patch, arrange the 25 squares in the desired pattern and number them with small sticky labels, so that you will know the correct order in which to join them.

I number the squares along the rows, so that the first row is 1-5, the second row 6-10, and so on. Stick the label in the center of the square so that it is nowhere

Numbering the squares.

near the seam allowance. Join the squares in pairs 1-2, 3-4, 6-7, 8-9, etc., and then join the odd ones, 5 onto 3-4, 10 onto 8-9, etc. Next, complete the rows, joining 1-2 to 3-4-5, 6-7 to 8-9-10, and so on. Remove the labels except for the first one in each row so that you can still identify the row. Avoid ironing them, since they may leave a sticky residue on the fabric. Press the seam allowances of all the even rows in one direction, and those of the odd

ABOVE: Miles pieces his numbered squares.

RIGHT: Katie adds a border to a 25-patch.

rows in the other direction. Then, when you join the rows, the seams will butt together nicely and lie flat. Join the rows in pairs, square #1 next to #6, and #11 next to #16. Join these two sets and then add the final row.

When the 25-patch is complete, press all the seams joining the rows in the same direction. When you add the border, press the seams away from the center field and toward the border.

Use these same principles when you join any sets of pieced square units.

Strip Piecing, Four-patches, Nine-patches, and Multiple Strips

Strip piecing is the technique in which strips of fabric are cut, and joined lengthwise. The joined strips may then be counter-cut to make units for the quilt block or top. Not only does this create very accurately sized pieces, but it also saves you an enormous amount of time, especially when multiple strips are involved.

To practice strip piecing, make some 4-patch units. Cut two 2½" strips, one in light, and one in dark fabric (see instructions for rotary cutting, page 15). Cut across the width of the fabric from selvage to selvage, then cut the strips in half so you have pieces about 20" long. Join the dark and the light strips and press, setting the seam first and then pressing the seam allowance toward the dark fabric. Press from the right

ABOVE: Alicen presses strips.

LEFT: Counter-cutting the strips for 4-patches.

ABOVE: *Bradford sews 4-patches.*

RIGHT: *Alicen counter-cuts to make 9-patches.*

side and make sure the seam line is straight and there are no folds. You can gently pull one end as you iron, to help straighten it and make it lie flat.

Counter-cut the strips 2½".

To make the 4-patches, join two of the pieces. Since the seam allowance is pressed toward the dark fabric, the seams at the intersection will butt up precisely, and the seam allowances on the two pieces will fall in opposing directions as described and illustrated above. Pin the pieces before you sew, making sure you have

at least one pin at the intersection where the seams butt. Sew and press the seam to one side.

To make 9-patches, two sequences of three strips are joined together, and then counter-cut.

In the Rail Fence quilt (see page 111), four long strips are joined and then cut into square units. If strip piecing were not used, you would need to cut four separate rectangles for every square unit. This would be far more time consuming for both the cutting and the sewing.

Cutting four strips for the Rail Fence.

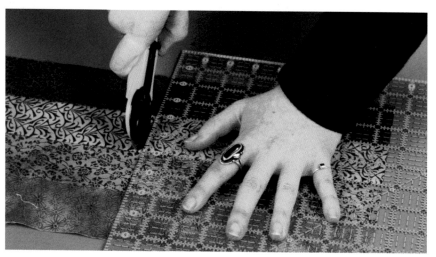

Corner Triangles

Corner triangles are made by cutting squares, marking them with a fine mechanical pencil (0.5mm lead) on the wrong side with a diagonal line corner-to-corner, and sewing along the marked line. This is a technique to sew the bias edges of triangular pieces together before cutting on the bias, and the triangles are accurate and easy to make. The corner triangle differs from the half-square triangle, in that each square only yields one triangle and you sew on the marked diagonal line. It is sewn onto a larger square or rectangle. Once the seam is stitched, trim away the corner seam allowance, and then press the seam allowance toward the darkest fabric. Some people like to press the squares in half diagonally and sew long the fold line, but in my experience, a pencil line is much easier to see. In this book, corner triangles are used for the Bowtie and Snowball patterns (sewn onto larger squares) and in the Star (two squares sewn onto each rectangle). The rectangles may also be used to make Flying Geese units.

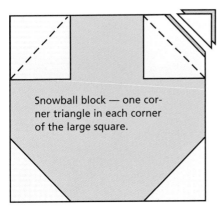

Snowball block — one corner triangle in each corner of the large square.

Use corner triangles for the Snowball block (at left), and Star points and Flying Geese (below).

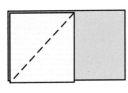
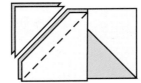
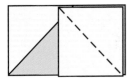
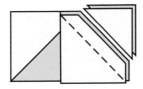
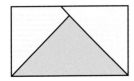

Star Points and Flying Geese — two corner triangles sewn onto a rectangle.

Half-Square Triangles

Half-square triangles are triangles made by dividing squares in half diagonally. The long edges of these right-angled triangles are bias edges. Bias edges stretch easily and may become misshapen. In this method of piecing, the half-square triangles are joined into squares without cutting the bias edge until after the seam has been sewn. Squares are cut and sewn, not triangles. Cut a square of each of the two triangle fabrics ⅞" larger than the finished size of the square unit you want to make (to allow for the seam allowances around the triangles). For example, in the 9" Shoo Fly block the finished size of the half-square triangle units is 3", so the original squares of the triangle fabrics are cut 3⅞". Draw a diagonal line using a fine mechanical pencil (0.5mm lead) from corner to corner on the backside of the lighter of the two squares. Put the two squares right sides together and sew two ¼" seams, one on each side of the line. Pin the squares in the corners away from the line, to stabilize them as you sew. If you find it hard to sew a ¼" seam accurately on each side of the centerline, you can draw the stitching lines in pencil and simply sew along them. After you have sewn both seams, cut along the center pencil line and open up the pieced squares. Each set of

Harrison sews half-square triangle units.

squares yields two half-square triangle units. Press the seam allowance toward the darkest fabric. If you are concerned about the accuracy of your ¼" seam allowance, cut the squares slightly larger, sew as instructed, and then trim the half-square triangle units to the precise size, being careful to maintain the triangle points in the corners.

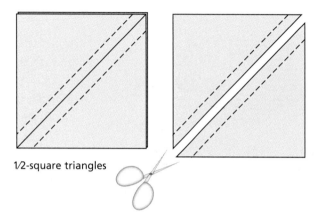

1/2-square triangles

Quarter-Square Triangles

Quarter-square triangles are made by cutting squares diagonally into quarters. This time the long edge of the triangle is on the straight grain and the two short sides are both bias edges. Thus, when these triangles are joined to make a square unit, the outer edge of the square is straight grain and all the bias edges are sewn. Start by making half-square triangle units as described above, cut them in half diagonally and then join them in the appropriate pairs to make the quarter-square triangle square units. Alternatively, instead of cutting them in half, repeat the half-square triangle process, drawing a diagonal line and stitching ¼" on either side. Make sure that you put the two opposite triangles right sides together when you do this (i.e., the darker next to the lighter and vice versa—the seam should butt nicely along the diagonal line). This time, the original squares should be cut 1¼" larger than the finished square unit (to allow for the seam allowances around the triangles). For example, in the Ohio Star (page 95), the finished square unit is 6½", so the squares are cut 7¾".

Layne cuts half-square triangle units in half and matches them to make quarter-square triangle units.

Crazy Patchwork

Crazy Patchwork blocks are made from irregularly shaped pieces put together in a random way. You can make attractive blocks using leftover scraps from other projects. Play around with different colors and have fun experimenting. Try to include a variety of colors and values in the block. Remember that using complementary colors will make the colors look more vibrant. Joining them with black or dark-colored sashing will also intensify them. I do not recommend making these for your initial project. First gain some experience and confidence with regular piecing and rotary cutting.

The Crazy Patchwork pillow (page 59) and doll quilt projects (page 100) both use 5½" (6" unfinished) blocks so you need to create a piece of patchwork large enough to cut out a 6" square. Start with any triangle and add irregular shaped pieces with straight edges onto it at any angle. Each time a new piece is added, trim off any excess seam allowance and press the seam allowance toward that piece. You will soon discover that if you add skinny pieces you will need a lot of them to make the block. After three pieces are sewn together, place a 6" square ruler over the patchwork to see where to add the next piece. You can also see what shape to cut it. Usually about five pieces are needed to make the patchwork large enough. Turn the 6" square ruler to the angle you like best, making sure there are no raw edges inside the 6" square. It looks better if you avoid having the outer seams parallel to the edge of the block. If there is rather a large piece down one side, simply sew on another piece at any angle over part of it. This will improve the look of the block. Hold the 6" square ruler firmly while you cut around it to make your 6" square. This part can be a little tricky since cuts may be at odd angles. Take extra care so that the ruler does not slip. A 6" x 24" or 6" x 12" ruler may be used if you do not have a 6" square.

Crazy patchwork pillow.

French Seams

French seams are seams sewn twice so that the raw edge of the first seam is completely enclosed. They provide extra strength and there are no raw edges exposed to fray when they are washed. In quilts, every seam is enclosed and so French seams are not necessary. In this book, they are used in the construction of the tote bags and pillowcases.

Place the wrong sides of the fabric together and sew a scant ¼" seam allowance. Press the seam and then turn the fabric so that the right sides are together and the sewn seam is along the edge. Press again, being careful that the seam is on the very edge and that there are no extra folds of fabric. Change the machine foot to a regular foot and sew the larger ⅜" second seam starting and ending with three or four back-stitches. When you press it and turn it right sides out there should be no raw edges hanging through the seam.

right side of fabric

First seam, scant ¼".

French seams

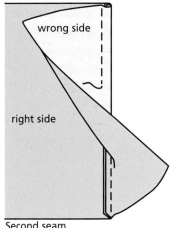

wrong side

right side

Second seam
⅜" seam, use regular
foot on sewing machine

Assembling Blocks and Adding Borders

Once you have made your quilt blocks, there are all sorts of options for assembling them. If you look through the projects in this book, you will see some of the variations. Detailed piecing instructions are provided for each project. The way in which you assemble your patchwork will dramatically affect the appearance of your quilt. Good fabric choices to frame or sash the blocks and add outer borders will greatly enhance the look of the quilt. I often make my blocks before I decide how to put them together. Then, when the blocks are completed, I can audition different fabrics to see which I like the best. I use my quilt wall to try out different arrangements, or the floor for a large quilt top. You can take your blocks to the fabric store and lay them out next to a variety of colors and values. There is usually no shortage of people around to offer their opinions and help you. Here are some ideas:

- Set the blocks squarely and adjacent (see red and white Bowtie, page 88, calico 4 Block Sampler, page 98).
- Set the blocks with sashing strips in between (see Bowties on yellow background, page 89).
- Set the blocks with sashing strips and cornerstones at the sashing intersections (see brown and blue Bowties, page88).
- Set the blocks with pieced sashing strips (see Ramona's Milky Way, page 120).
- Frame each block and then add sashing strips (see Sophie's Family Quilt, page 74).
- Frame each block and add sashing strips and cornerstones at the sashing intersections (see 4 Block Sampler batik quilt, page 99).
- Set the blocks on point in any of the ways above.
- You can use any of the project patterns, or design your own. When designing your own quilt layout, consider how big you want the end product. Use graph paper to draw the finished size to scale, and then don't forget to add the seam allowances when you cut the pieces.

When you add sashing strips onto blocks, always press the seam allowances away from the blocks and toward the sashing strips. The same applies for frames and outer borders. If you add cornerstone squares to the intersections of the sashing strips, press the seam

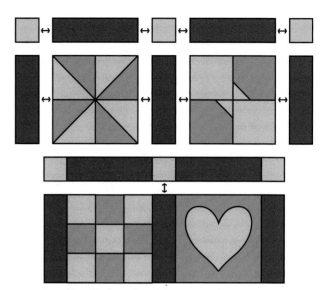

Assembling blocks with sashing strips and cornerstones.

allowances toward the sashing strips. Then, when you join all the pieces, the seam allowances will butt in opposing directions and the seams will lie smoothly at the intersections.

Use the same piecing principles as for piecing squares (see page 23); that is, always piece in an order that allows you to sew in straight lines without insetting any seams. Assemble your blocks in rows with their sashing strips, and then join the rows together with the sashing strips that separate the rows.

For frames and borders, first sew on two opposite sides, and then join the other two sides. Measure and calculate the correct sizes carefully to include the seam allowances. For example, to add a 2" frame around an 8" block (finished sizes), cut the two side frame strips 2½" x 8½" and the top and bottom strips 2½" x 12½".

When you add borders onto a quilt top, measure the distance across the center and not the edge (which tends to distort) of the patchwork, and use this to calculate the size of the strips to cut for the border. If the edge is a little larger than the center, you will need to ease the extra in, distributing it evenly along the entire seam length. Pin each end and gently pull to see how much extra you have. Find the center points on both bits of fabric and pin, and then put pins halfway between the center and the ends. Add more pins at the mid-points between pins to gradually work in the excess fabric. When you sew, place the longer of the two fabrics underneath, and then it will be easier to ease in the excess.

Ramona adds the border to a pillow top.

A discrepancy of more than about ½" over a distance of about 24" will be difficult to accommodate. Double-check your calculations and the accuracy of the piecing of the center area of the quilt top. If you simply cut the border strip the same size as a stretched edge, you will make the quilt even more misshapen and it will have wavy edges that do not hang squarely. Taking the time to tackle this stage carefully and precisely is well worthwhile, even though you may be a little over-eager to finish the project!

If a border is longer than the full width of the fabric (42"), you have two choices. It can be pieced, which is fine for many monochromatic or small-print fabrics since the join is not very visible. Alternatively, it can be cut in one piece, lengthwise from the fabric, in which case much more fabric is required. For example, for four 3" x 50" border strips, at least 50" is needed to avoid joining strips. If the border is pieced, five full-width 3" strips are needed (the fifth is divided into four 10" strips to lengthen the other four), and only 15" of fabric is required. However, when the cuts are made lengthwise, there is plenty of extra fabric that can be used for other parts of the quilt such as the binding or in a pieced back. To use the fabric featured in the center field of the quilt, cut the border strips first to make sure you have enough length before you make cuts across the width of the fabric.

Quilt Backs

Quilt backs for small quilts are easy. Simply cut the back a little larger, at least 1½" on each side, than the quilt top. Allow this extra on all quilt backs in case of quilt uptake or distortion during quilting. If you cut the back the same size as the quilt, it is harder to align it exactly with the quilt top (batting is in between). Also, after quilting, you may find that the back doesn't come all the way to edge of the top. This causes problems when you bind the quilt. The excess quilt backing

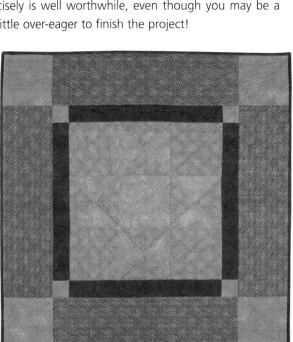

Topside and back of Bright Star (Ohio Star quilt, page 113).

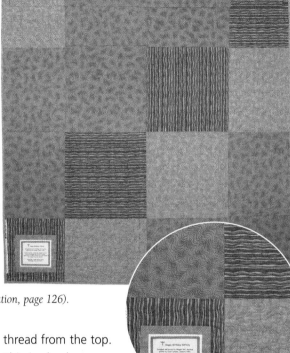

Topside and back of Happy Birthday Infinity (Log Cabin variation, page 126).

and batting is trimmed after the binding is attached by machine, and before the binding is stitched to the back by hand.

For quilts larger than 42" wide, the quilt back has to be pieced, unless you purchase wider fabric (a small variety of 90" and 108" wide fabrics is available). It is possible to economize on the yardage by careful planning. Long bits of fabric are needed for border strips, but the leftover long pieces can be used to piece the quilt back, so that you don't have to buy two full quilt lengths of the backing fabric. A pieced back can look attractive on a lap quilt, but stick to large pieces to minimize the seam allowances (so the quilt back stays flat, is easy to quilt, and does not pucker when quilted). Using fabrics that appear in the quilt top, or that match or complement them is recommended, but for a wall hanging this is not important. Here are two examples of pieced lap quilt backs; both sides of the quilts are shown. Since I didn't have enough yardage of any single fabric for the entire back, I pieced together a variety of fabrics from the smaller bits on hand.

Unsewing or Reverse Sewing

You will make mistakes—everyone does! To undo your sewing, use a seam ripper to cut through every third stitch, being careful not to catch the fabric. The back thread will pull away easily in one long piece, and then you can remove the small fragments of cut thread from the top. This is also known as "the frog stitch": rip-it, rip-it, rip-it!

Alex uses a seam ripper.

Quilts & Blankets

Preemie Baby or Doll Blankets

Many of the small quilts featured in this book are made with flannel backs and have no batting. They are not technically quilts, but they make wonderful receiving blankets for premature babies or dolls and stuffed animal blankets.

Instead of sandwiching layers as for a quilt, sew the flannel back and the patchwork top right sides together all the way around, leaving a gap of 4" to 5" (envelope style). Use a regular foot on the sewing machine to sew with a ⅜" seam allowance. Start and end the stitching with two or three backstitches. Trim away the excess flannel and clip the corners by cutting off a little triangle in the seam allowance.

Turn the blanket right side out, and use a blunt pencil or a crotchet hook to gently poke out the corners. Press it carefully, turning in the seam allowance at the

Grace pins and sews her blanket top and flannel back together.

Trim away the excess flannel and cut off the corners.

Grace and Ramona turn their blankets right side out.

Donna topstitches her blanket.

gap. Whipstitch the gap closed by hand, or sew with the machine very close to the edge of the blanket (⅛" or less) all the way around the outside. Add more stitching to hold the two layers together. This can be minimal since the flannel back and regular cotton top cling together nicely. The stitching may be decorative. Use shiny and variegated thread to enhance the appearance of the little blanket; these threads are fun to use! Since you are only sewing through two layers of fabric, there is no need to use a special walking foot or to adjust the machine in any way. This successfully conveys the concept of quilting stitches, without having the entire quilt sandwich.

Some of the small quilts have batting, but are tied and have no binding on the edge. These are technically comforters and not quilts, since they do not have quilting stitches. They are constructed in the same way, envelope style, as the little blankets, but the batting is included. Place the batting on a flat sur-face, then lay the quilt back right side up on top of it. Then put the quilt top right side down over the backing and batting. Pin and sew as for the blanket, placing the batting next to the feed dogs on the machine.

Clip the corners, turn, and close the gap as described above. Tie or add quilting stitches to hold the three layers together.

Flannel-backed blankets.

From Quilt Top to Quilt

Once the patchwork top is completed, add the batting and backing to make the quilt sandwich, sew it all together with quilting stitches, and finish the edge. This involves several steps, which can sometimes take as long, or longer, as the piecing of the quilt top. The three layers are basted or pinned together until the quilting stitches are completed. The basting is then removed and the edge of the quilt is finished with either the addition of a binding, or by using the top or backing fabric to enclose it. Detailed instructions for all these steps are provided below.

Selecting the Batting

There are many different types of batting on the market and choosing the appropriate one may be a little daunting. However, it is much easier if you know what questions to ask and have some basic knowledge. Read the packaging carefully. It will tell you what the batting is made of, the height of the loft, and how far apart you can stitch the lines of quilting. Store assistants should be able to advise you if have any questions.

Do you want polyester, cotton, or cotton/poly blended batting?

The advantage of polyester batting is that it holds together well, so that you can leave large gaps between your lines of quilting stitches or your ties. But, if you are making a lap quilt and you want it to be warm, cotton is warmer; a good compromise in this case is 80 percent cotton, 20 percent polyester blend. The cotton keeps you warm and the polyester bonds the cotton together so that your quilting lines can be relatively far apart. If you go for 100 percent cotton, it will be even warmer but you will need to quilt closer together. Some cotton battings contain a scrim, which is a very thin mesh of plastic to hold the cotton together so that the quilting stitches can be further apart. These battings are great for wall hangings, but are not as warm as the cottons without the scrim. You may have to read the small print or ask the retailer to find out whether or not the batting has a scrim. If you are going to hand quilt your work, avoid polyester battings (80 percent cotton/20 percent polyester is OK)

and cotton battings that have a scrim. Wool and silk battings are also available, but they are more expensive and I do not recommend using these for beginning projects.

What height of loft should you use?

The loft is the thickness of the batting. It can dramatically affect the appearance of the quilt. High lofts are poofy and lower lofts will lie flatter when stitched. For machine quilting, I usually use low, or sometimes medium, loft batting. The polyester batts tend to have higher lofts and poof out more than cotton, but you can find a wide range in both. Tied quilts look attractive with higher lofts and polyester is easy to use and appropriate for the little tied quilts, and the tied 4-patch lap quilt.

Some types of batting shrink when they are washed. Check the directions on the packaging. It may be desirable to pre-wash the batting before you use it.

The quality of batting has improved tremendously in recent years and the newer cotton batts hold together much better than previously. The choice is large and you can even purchase adhesive batting that can be ironed into the quilt sandwich and does not need basting (not recommended for hand quilting). Remember the basic questions of batting content, loft, and the minimum distance for quilting lines, and you should be able to make an informed decision.

Basting the "Quilt Sandwich"

Basting stitches hold the three layers of the quilt together until the quilting is completed, and are then removed. The quilt back and batting should always be at least 1½" larger on each side than the quilt top, to allow for any uptake or distortion during quilting. The excess is trimmed after the binding has been attached.

Baste with long running (basting) stitches, safety pins, or by using a basting gun with plastic tacks. Spray can adhesives or iron-on batting are also options. I prefer traditional basting stitches. The basting takes longer but the stitches don't rust like some safety pins, or get in the way while you are quilting. Basting a large quilt is much more enjoyable if it is made into a social occasion with a reward of tea, or dessert at the end!

1. Press the quilt top and the quilt back (the seams on the quilt back may be pressed open).
2. Lay the quilt back flat, wrong side up, on a table (with a non-scratch surface or one you don't mind scratching), hard floor, or low-pile carpet. I use a table for small quilts and baste large quilts on the floor.
3. Tape the quilt back to the surface with masking tape, or use T-pins on a carpet. Secure the opposing sides, working from the center out to the corners. Do the same for the other two sides. Make sure the quilt back is perfectly flat. It should be taut but not stretched so that it is distorted.

Use a spoon to baste.

4. Place the batting on top of the backing. Gently smooth it out so that there are no wrinkles.
5. Place the quilt top, right side up, over the batting. Position the quilt top centrally over the quilt back, leaving a margin of quilt back and batting exposed around each edge (at least 1½"). Check that it is perfectly flat and square. Straight seams sometimes appear a little crooked and the quilt top may be gently manipulated to align them correctly.
6. If you are working on the floor, T-pin the quilt top in the same way as the quilt back. On a table, put safety pins in the corners and the center of each side through all three layers. Use a dessert or grapefruit spoon to help lift the end of the pin up from the surface so you can easily secure it.
7. Use quilting or regular thread, a large needle, and a spoon to lift the needle from the surface. Baste a grid of large running stitches all over the quilt. Start in the middle of one side of the quilt and baste all

the way across. You may knot the thread or make a couple of backstitches at the beginning. Take four or five stitches before pulling the thread all the way through. This saves time, especially if your thread is long. The second line of basting stitches should be about a hand's width away from the first. Continue basting the lines until you are near the edges of the quilt. Then baste at right angles, creating a grid of stitches.

8. Remove the tape or pins from the edges and baste all the way around the quilt ½" to 1" from the edges.

The basting stitches remain until the quilting is completed. Remove all of them except those around the perimeter of the quilt, which stay until the binding is attached.

Quilting

The quilting stitches are a vital component of a quilt since they hold the three layers of the quilt sandwich together. They can also greatly enhance the appearance of the quilt. Quilting stitch patterns show up particularly well on solid colors, or pale monochromatic fabrics and small prints. The quilting may be stitched by machine (commercially or on a regular machine), or by hand, and should be of an even density over the entire quilt. Quilting lines may follow or echo the geometric piecing pattern, or be completely different. I've made simple suggestions for the projects in this book. The action of quilting takes up some of the quilt top, so you may find that, after quilting, your quilt is a little smaller (up to 1" to 2" on a large quilt).

Machine Quilting

For straight line quilting, use a dual-feed walking foot on your machine. The walking foot moves the three layers through the machine evenly and helps prevent tucks and bumps. For free-motion machine quilting, drop or cover the feed dogs on the machine and set the stitch length and width dials to zero. Use a darning/embroidery foot. The way you move the fabric and the speed with which you run the motor will determine the stitch length and pattern. For help with machine quilting, refer to Maurine Noble's book *Machine Quilting Made Easy!* or take a class. It

Sophie uses the walking foot for straight line quilting.

Sophie practices free-motion machine quilting.

requires a little practice, but after two or three hours, you will be proficient enough to tackle your quilt.

Straight line quilting "in the ditch" is a method often used. "In the ditch" means right next to the seam line on the side without the seam allowance, so that the stitching line is barely visible. It is actually rather difficult to do this accurately, although many quilters are under the illusion that this is an easy option. My preferred method, and one which is very simple for quilters of all ages, is to stitch with a serpentine stitch along the seam line. This snake-like stitch curves backwards and forwards across the seam line, and is very forgiving. It also looks attractive, especially in variegated thread. Use it diagonally across blocks and to make a grid. A good example of this stitching may be seen on the Family Pets quilt, page 75. Straight line quilting is fine down the center of a strip or border, or diagonally across a block like a 9-patch, but I suggest avoiding sewing in the ditch. When straight line quilting, you can start and stop with tiny stitches which will not come out when you clip the thread ends.

Free-motion quilting is great fun but, as I already mentioned, it requires practice. Sophie, my 12-year-old quilting buddy, loves it. She quilted the background in this way on her Spring Chickens, see page 69, and on Sophie's Family Quilt, page 74. If you try this method, always begin by bringing the bobbin thread up to the top of the quilt so that it does not become tangled and resemble a bird's nest on the back. Take a needle and darn all the loose ends into the batting when you have finished quilting. If you cut the ends without doing this, your quilting stitches may come out.

When the quilting is finished, remove all the basting stitches except for those around the edge. These help to stabilize the edge while you add the binding. Remove them after the binding has been machine stitched and before it is hand stitched to the back.

Commercial Quilting

If you decide that you would like your work professionally quilted, there are plenty of machine quilters around to accept your business. My good friend, Wanda Rains (Rainy Day Quilts), quilted several of the pieces in this book using a long arm sewing machine. The long arm machine has a 10-foot or larger frame and a free moving quilting arm that can be moved over the surface of the quilt. Bed quilts may be quilted in about five hours. I encourage you to try to quilt your own quilts, but the larger the quilt, the more difficult it is to handle using a regular sewing machine. If you are short of time, or have a large quilt, commercial quilting is a good option. Be warned that you may need to book your slot well in advance with the quilter. The commercial quilter should be able to advise you on the type of batting and supply it for you. They may also be able to furnish the backing fabric. If you provide your own quilt back, you may need to allow extra inches around each edge for it to be attached to the frame—check with the quilter. Before you drop off your quilt, thi0nk about the quilting pattern you would like. Wanda and I work together and discuss the quilting patterns in detail. The quilter should be able to make several suggestions for you. Often, an all-over repeated pattern is used, but a good quilter can custom design anything you want, making a variety of patterns on different areas of the quilt.

Sophie hand quilting.

Hand Quilting

Only one of the quilts in this book is hand quilted: the Christmas Ohio Star, page 96. The plain background squares have quilted wreaths and the quilting in the star simply follows the geometric shapes.

Children love to quilt by hand. Use a 14" embroidery hoop to secure the area, (not taut, but with some slack), to be quilted. Don't give children larger hoops because their hands won't be able to reach the center underneath. For group projects, a quilting frame is fun and they will enjoy sitting, chatting, and stitching. Other necessary supplies are a thimble (one that fits!), Betweens (quilting needles, Sizes 7 to 10), and quilting thread. Beeswax to make the thread run through the fabric more easily and reduce knotting is optional.

Keep the quilting designs simple. Here are some suggestions that require no markings:

1. Quilt around the edge of each block, in or near the ditch (avoid quilting through the seam allowance).
2. Use masking tape as a guide to quilt ¼" away from the seams on geometric patterns.
3. Quilt 9-patch squares with diagonal lines from corner to corner (use strips of masking tape for stitching guides).
4. Quilt around the outside of shapes like hearts.

If you need to mark the quilt, use a fine lead pencil (Ultimate Marking Pencil for Quilters), a Berol silver pencil, or chalk pencils. Many stencils are available with attractive quilting patterns that can be marked on the surface of the quilt.

Quilting needles are small for children to handle and thread. Use Size 7 at first. Children will probably need help threading the needle initially. Use the following steps as a guide for hand quilting.

1. Thread the needle with a piece of quilting thread approximately 18" long and make a knot close to the end.

2. Bury the knot in the batting by inserting the needle into the middle layer about 1½" from the starting point. Move it through the batting, bringing it to the surface at the starting point. Pull the thread until the knot and tail pop through the top of the quilt and disappear into the batting.

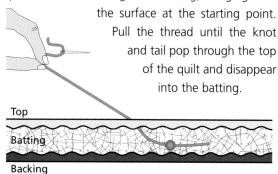

3. Move the needle with a rocking motion, stitching through all three layers of the quilt.

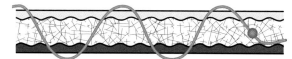

Stitch through all three layers.

4. End off by knotting the thread twice within 1" of the quilt surface, and burying the knots in the batting as you did at the start.

Using a thimble is awkward at first, but necessary.

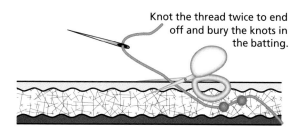

Knot the thread twice to end off and bury the knots in the batting.

Work from the top of the quilt, with the needle in one hand and the other hand under the quilt to push the needle up as it comes through to the back of the quilt. There is a tendency to flip over work in a hoop, or creep under the quilt frame to catch the needle underneath! The first stitch is the most difficult. You must push up the point of the needle from below with the index finger as soon as it penetrates the back. Then use the thimble to push the needle as it moves up and down through the quilt. Take two or three stitches at a time, but no more. For some children this is difficult, so they may need to take just one stitch at a time.

Tying

Tying is a fast and easy substitute for quilting stitches. Technically, a tied quilt is really a comforter (quilts must have quilting stitches). Quilts to be tied may be basted with safety pins. Use embroidery floss or pearl cotton in a color or variety of colors that complement the quilt top.

1. Mark the positions for the ties, spacing them evenly no more than 6" apart.

2. Using a large needle, take a small stitch through all the layers at the position for the tie. Pull the thread through and leave a tail of 3" to 4". Continue in this way, threading the needle again as necessary. Cut the threads midway between the stitches.

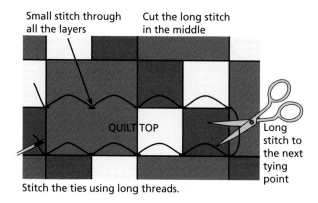

Stitch the ties using long threads.

3. Use the tails to firmly tie square knots over the stitches (right over left and under, then left over right and under). Check the knots to make sure they are secure and tight.

4. Trim the tails to the desired length.

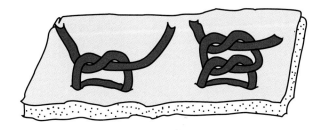

Buttons, Beads, and Charms

You may also use buttons, beads, or charms to secure the three layers of the quilt; they add a decorative touch. These look particularly attractive on crazy quilts, and may be used in combination with ties; see page 100.

Binding the Quilt

Binding strips may be cut on the straight grain of the fabric unless the quilt has curved or irregular edges. I recommend a French (double) binding since it is strong and durable and finishes the quilt with a firm edge.

1. Calculate the number of binding strips needed by measuring the perimeter of the quilt and dividing by 40 for fabric 42" wide.

2. Cut 2½" wide binding strips. For flannel, I recommend 3" strips.

3. Cut the ends of the strips at 45-degree angles and join them together.

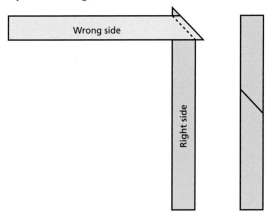

4. Press the seams open and press the binding in half lengthwise with the wrong sides together.

5. The quilt should be quilted, but still have basting stitches ½" to 1" from the outer edge. Align the raw edge of the binding with the raw edge of the quilt top. Start stitching about 10" below a corner, leaving a tail of 6" to 8" of binding for joining at the end. Use a walking foot for the best results. Stop ¼" from the first corner, make three or four backstitches, and remove the quilt from the sewing machine.

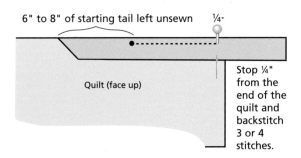

6. Rotate the quilt a quarter turn and fold the binding straight up, away from the corner, making a 45-degree angle fold. Bring the binding straight down in line with the next raw edge to be sewn. The top fold of the binding should be even with the edge just sewn.

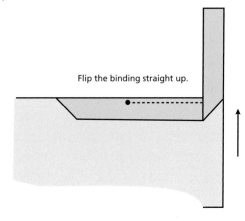

Flip the binding straight up.

7. Start stitching with backstitches right to the edge of the top fold, then stitch until you reach the next corner. Stop and backstitch. Continue for all sides of the quilt.

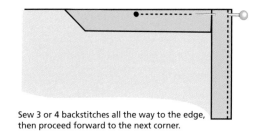

Sew 3 or 4 backstitches all the way to the edge, then proceed forward to the next corner.

8. Fold the binding at the corner as previously described and pin it by the top fold.

9. Trim the end of the binding to join it with a 45-degree angle seam to the 6" to 8" tail you left at the start. Open the binding ends and draw a pencil line at 45 degrees where they join. Cut the tail ½" away from the line to accommodate the seam allowance. Stitch the binding ends together and finger press the seam open.

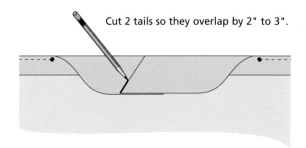

Cut 2 tails so they overlap by 2" to 3".

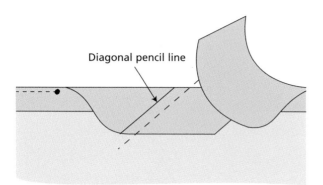

Diagonal pencil line

Cut the ending tail ½" longer than the diagonal pencil line.

10. Stitch the binding down, beginning with the back-stitches at the corner and continuing until you meet the starting point.
11. Remove the basting stitches.
12. Use a rotary cutter or scissors to trim the excess batting and backing flush with the quilt top and binding raw edge. The binding should be stuffed evenly with batting, so trim carefully.
13. Bring the folded edge of the binding to the back of the quilt so it covers the machine stitching line. Hand stitch it down with a blind stitch, pinning a small section at a time to hold it in place as you sew. Use thread that matches the binding rather than the quilt back.
14. Miter the corners by folding the unstitched binding from the next side over to form the 45-degree angle (it's rather like wrapping up a parcel).

Another way to bind is to machine sew the binding onto the back of the quilt, then bring it to the front and top stitch with a decorative machine stitch, as in Sophie's lap quilt (page 109).

A third way is to fold the edge of the back of the quilt to the front and stitch it down. Make sure the backing is a coordinating fabric. Cut the batting flush with the edge of the quilt top. Cut the back at least 1" larger on each side than the quilt top. Fold over ⅜" on each edge and press. Bring this folded edge forward and pin it to the quilt top, then stitch it down using a machine with a walking foot or a hand blind stitch. Sew the two longest opposite sides first, then fold and sew the other two sides with a miter at the corners so no raw edges are exposed. This sounds like an easy option, but it is actually quite difficult to make neat and tidy.

Sophie uses a walking foot to attach French binding.

Making a Label

Labeling the quilt is an important finishing touch. Years from now, people will be curious about who made the quilt, and when, and where. You can embroider, write with fabric markers, or print a label from a computer. Use a pale fabric so that the words show clearly. If you are using markers, iron freezer paper to the back to stabilize the fabric while you are writing. To print from a computer, use a laser jet printer on specially treated, paper-backed fabric. Most brands need to be heat-set with an iron after printing. Follow the directions given on the product you choose. Include the following information on your label: quilt title, names of all the participants, date, and location.

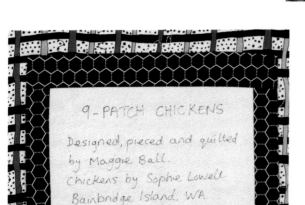

Handmade and computer-generated labels.

You may add a narrow colored frame to the label to make it look more distinctive. Use a blind hemming stitch in thread matching the frame to attach the label to the back of the quilt. I usually position the label in a lower corner of the quilt where it is easy to see by lifting the corner when the quilt is hanging.

Hanging the Quilt

An easy way to hang a quilt is to attach a sleeve to the back along the top edge. The sleeve is a fabric tube wide enough to accommodate a dowel. You can hang the dowel on hooks or suspend fishing line from museum-style hangers on the wall. Use plain muslin or a fabric that matches the quilt back to make a hanging sleeve.

1. For a 4" wide sleeve, cut a fabric strip 8½" wide and 2" shorter than the quilt top.
2. Turn ½" to the wrong side of each short end and machine stitch.
3. Fold the sleeve in half lengthwise with the right sides together, and machine stitch the raw edges. Turn right side out and press.
4. Pin the sleeve to the quilt back at the top, 1" below the binding.

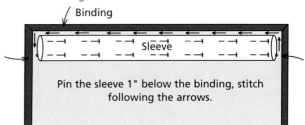

Pin the sleeve 1" below the binding, stitch following the arrows.

Stop sewing 1" from the lower edge of the sleeve.

5. Blind stitch the sleeve to the quilt, taking care that your stitches don't pass all the way through the quilt and show on the front. Start 1" from the lower edge of one end of the sleeve, stitch across the top, and down the other edge, stopping 1" from the bottom. Now you have sewn the sleeve on three sides.
6. Reposition the fold in the sleeve and the pins. Move the sleeve up so that the top fold is just below the binding and pin it in place.

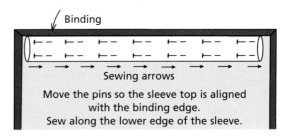

Move the pins so the sleeve top is aligned with the binding edge.
Sew along the lower edge of the sleeve.

7. Blind stitch along the bottom edge. Remove the pins. This method eliminates any bulging on the front of the quilt around the dowel.
8. Hang the quilt and enjoy!

You may hang small quilts using fabric or ribbon loops (see Wall Hangings, page 67). Simply sew the loops to the backside of the quilt making sure they are all the same length.

Other Techniques

Most of this book focuses on pieced patchwork projects, but there are other ways to make decorative images on fabric. Some projects use fusible appliqué, and one or two quilts include illustrations on fabric, paint, and computer images. I have included these so that you can take the ideas and techniques and adapt them for your own creative endeavors. There are many more examples in my first book, *Creative Quilting with Kids* (Krause Publications, 2001).

Fusible Appliqué

You can use fusible appliqué in a variety of ways. Several projects use relatively large shapes such as hands and hearts, and you may use pieces of any size or shape ("snippets") to create pictures. Leftover scraps are great for snippet projects. Choose pale-colored fabric for the background and bright colors for the appliqué pieces to ensure that the pictures and shapes are bold and clear (see pictorial quilts, page 67).

Sophie draws, cuts, and fuses a heart.

Sophie hand embroiders with blanket stitch around the heart.

The technique of fusible appliqué relies on commercial adhesive webbing, bonded by heat, to stick appliqué pieces onto a background. My preference is for Steam-a-Seam 2, since the bonding is achieved in one step. The webbing is slightly tacky, so you can place an appliqué piece in position while other pieces are added. If, before bonding, you need to adjust the position of a piece, simply peel it away from the background and move it. When you have correctly arranged all the appliqué pieces, heat-bond them by placing a damp cloth over the appliqué and pressing with a hot iron, without moving the iron, for ten seconds.

Another advantage of Steam-a-Seam 2 is the ease of stitching through the layers smoothly, without the needle becoming coated in the adhesive. You can hand or machine embroider a blanket, or zigzag stitch around the edge of the shape, or machine embroider on top of the appliqué to embellish (see machine embroidered hearts, page 72).

Remember that if the appliqué shape is drawn on the paper backing, when it is cut out the image will be reversed—left hands will appear as right hands and vice versa. To solve this problem, you can draw the shape on freezer paper, iron it onto the right side of the fabric, and then add the Steam-a-Seam 2 to the back of the fabric before cutting out the shape.

The adhesive should withstand washing and wear and tear, but if you plan to wash it frequently, you should sew around the edge of the appliqué shapes with a blanket or zigzag stitch for additional stability.

Illustrations on Fabric

To draw pictures or write on fabric, use fabric markers and/or crayons. The markers are clean and easy to use, but crayons are useful for coloring in large areas. Choose a pale colored fabric so that the illustrations stand out clearly. Unbleached muslin, pastel solids, and pale monochromatic prints work well. The illustrations may be used for patchwork pillows or decorative wall hangings. Use markers to make a written label for the backside of your quilt.

To prepare the fabric, iron a piece of freezer paper (shiny, waxed-side down) to the wrong side. This stabilizes it while you draw or write. Not only does the freezer paper prevent the fabric from shifting and distorting while you draw or write, but you can draw the designs on the paper and trace them directly onto fabric. You can make, erase, and redraw pencil drawings until they are just right. Place the fabric backed with freezer paper on a light table, an overhead projector, or tape it to a window, and trace the picture onto the fabric side.

Attach the freezer paper to the fabric by ironing the two together before you cut the blocks or panels. To do this, first press the fabric, then place the shiny side of the freezer paper down on the wrong side of the fabric and iron gently (cotton setting). The wax melts, attaching the freezer paper to the fabric. Turn it over to make sure the fabric is smooth and without wrinkles. If there are bumps, simply peel the freezer paper away when it is cool and try again. You may also press it from the fabric side. Cut the freezer paper backed fabric to the desired size. If the freezer paper starts to come off while you are drawing or writing, just iron it in place again.

Draw a ½" margin around the edge of the paper. Make sure that the illustration does not cross into this

Sophie draws on fabric.

margin, and then none of it will be devoured in a seam allowance when it is pieced into the quilt or pillow cover. Note that when you trace the image from the paper onto the fabric, it will be reversed. If you want to write on the fabric, trace the writing from a separate piece of paper or else it will be backwards! Remove the paper when the illustration is complete and recycle it for your next project.

All purpose craft ink for Fantastix is fun and easy to use. Use the Fantastix like markers and mix or water down the colors to create a variety of effects.

Embellish border strips or quilt blocks with rubber stamps. Use stamp pads with fabric ink and get creative! Ironing freezer paper to the backside of your fabric will keep it stable while you do the stamping. See page 55 for examples of illustrated patchwork pillows and page 74 for a wall hanging.

Reverse Stencils

Reverse stencil prints on fabric are made from homemade freezer paper stencils and fabric paint. Cut any shape out of freezer paper and iron it, waxed side down, onto a fabric block. Sponge paint the entire block with fabric paint, and then when the paint dries, peel away the freezer paper shape. The freezer paper prevents the paint from reaching the fabric and leaves a silhouette of the shape, hence it is a reverse stencil. See page 96 for a doll's blanket made with snowflake printed fabric. For further details on this technique, refer to my first book, *Creative Quilting with Kids* (Krause Publications, 2001).

Printing Computer Generated or Photocopied Images

Computer generated images of any kind may be printed using an inkjet printer on specially treated fabric, such as ColorPlus Fabrics, available at quilting or craft stores. Carefully feed the paper-backed fabric into your printer. Follow the directions provided by the manufacturer and experiment to create your own fabric from photographs, graphics, or drawings on your computer. The fabric may be included in any project; see page 75 for a wall hanging. Additionally, most large print shops can photocopy photographs onto fabric for you.

Section
2

Preemie baby blankets.

Patchwork and *Quilting* P·R·O·J·E·C·T·S

Now that you have absorbed all the basics described in Section One, you are ready to start sewing! The projects begin with the simplest and least time consuming, and progress to those that are larger and more ambitious.

I suggest that you begin by making a patchwork pillow or a simple little quilt before you attempt a lap quilt. If you already have some experience, by all means, dig straight into the big projects.

A supply list appears with each project, along with cutting sizes and general instructions. Please refer to Section One for all the detailed, technical "how to" instructions. The supply lists provide fabric requirements and assume that you have the basics, such as a sewing machine, thread, pins, rotary cutter, mat, and ruler (see page 10). There may be some variation in the finished size of the projects due to different finishing techniques (bound or envelope style). Quilting may affect the size, reducing it a little.

Here are some useful tips and reminders:

- Make sure your sewing machine is in good working order.
- Pre-wash and press all your fabrics.
- Read the project directions carefully and refer to Section One for details on the techniques before you start.
- Make notes on your project. Draw a sketch and record the positions of the different fabrics.
- Always use a consistent ¼" seam allowance, except when instructed otherwise.
- Block sizes refer to the finished size, unless specified as the unfinished size.
- Take extra care with long borders, measuring the center field of the quilt and adjusting the border length if necessary.
- Be realistic about your skill level and the length of the project you tackle.
- Savor the moment when you finish your project, and celebrate!

The projects include something for everyone: patchwork pillows, tote bags, pillow cases, wall hangings, little quilts, preemie baby receiving blankets, and lap quilts.

Patchwork Blocks

Patchwork blocks are fun to piece together for a variety of projects, such as pillows, to decorate tote bags, and in quilts of any size. Pieced blocks are those in which the patchwork shapes are cut out and sewn together. In appliqué blocks, a background block is cut, and then smaller pieces are attached. All of the appliqué projects in this book utilize heat-bonded fusible webbing to attach the pieces to the background.

I encourage you to improvise on the basic designs described on these pages by playing around with the 4-patch, 9-patch, or 16-patch units and rearranging them into your own patterns. The variety of options will amaze you, and you can have the satisfaction of creating your very own block.

Making Patchwork Blocks

Appendix 1 gives a block pattern summary, and Appendix 2 provides cutting sizes for the pieces for both 9" and 12" blocks. Appendix 1 groups the blocks according to type (4-patch, 9-patch, 16-patch, and appliqué). The 4-patch blocks may be divided into four equal squares (2 x 2), and the squares may be further subdivided into smaller squares, triangles, or rectangles. Likewise, 9-patch blocks may be divided into nine equal squares, and 16-patch blocks into 16 equal squares and, in both, the squares may be subdivided. The photographs show single blocks on pillows and illustrate the different patterns arranged according to the method of construction. Follow the instructions for accurate cutting, pinning, and piecing that is outlined in Section One, and don't forget to use a consistent ¼" seam allowance. Remember to sew in straight lines without insetting any seams. For each block, first construct the basic square units, join them in rows, and then join the rows, just like the Simple 4-patches and 9-patches.

Blocks Using Squares

Make the Simple 4-patch and Simple 9-patch blocks from squares pieced together. Join the squares in rows, and then sew the rows together to complete your block. See page 23 for instructions. To make multiple 4-patches or 9-patches, use the strip piecing method (page 25).

4-patch and 9-patch pillows.

Blocks Using Strip Piecing

Strip piecing saves cutting out all the individual shapes in the block. In the Double 4-patch, the small 4-patch units can be strip pieced. Cut each of the 9-patch units in London Stairs from two strips joined together. See page 25 for strip piecing instructions.

London Stairs and Double 4-patch pillows.

Blocks Using Corner Triangles

Blocks using corner triangles are the Bowtie and the Star. Instead of cutting out triangles, cut and sew squares diagonally in half. This makes piecing more accurate, since you do not have to align bias raw edges that tend to distort easily. See page 27 for instructions to make corner triangles.

Bowtie and Star pillows.

Blocks Using Half-Square Triangles

Patterns using half-square triangles provide plenty of options, since each unit may be oriented in four different ways simply by rotation. The Pinwheel, Sawtooth, Broken Dishes, Chevron, and Flying Geese are all 4-patch blocks made from four half-square triangle units. The photographs depict the Pinwheel and Broken Dishes. Refer to Appendix 1 to see the layout of the others. See page 27 for instructions to construct half-square triangles.

Broken Dishes pillow.

To design your own pattern using four half-square triangles, photocopy the 4-patch grids in Appendix 4 and color in the triangles. Make one of the triangles dark in color and the other light or contrasting. Cut out the square units and try rotating them to make different patterns. Alternatively, simply construct the four half-square triangles from fabric and then turn them and play until you find the pattern you like best.

For all the 9-patch blocks with triangles (Shoo Fly, Friendship Star, Contrary Wife, Wings in a Whirl, and Churn Dash), you can use the half-square triangle method. The Churn Dash also uses strip piecing for the units composed of two rectangles. The photographs show the Shoo Fly and the Churn Dash. Refer to Appendix 1 to see the layout of the others.

Pinwheel pillow.

Shoo Fly and Churn Dash pillows.

Designing Your Own Blocks

You can design your own blocks easily by using the 4-patch and 9-patch grids provided in Appendices 4 and 5. Color and cut out the squares. Mix and match to make your own 4-patch patterns. On the 9-patch, subdivide the squares into half-square triangles, quarter-square triangles, rectangles, or small squares. Alternatively, draw the finished size of the block to scale on graph paper. For a 9" 4-patch block, each unit is 4½", and for a 12" block, the unit size is 6". In the case of 9-patch blocks, the basic unit sizes are 3" and 4" for 9" and 12" blocks, respectively. Remember to add ¼" seam allowances before you cut the fabric and, if you are making half- or quarter-square triangles, refer to the instructions on pages 27 and 28 for guidance on the cutting sizes. You may divide the square units up any way you like and easily create unique patterns. If you are worried about calculating the sizes of the pieces, use the components already provided and just draw a rough sketch. For example, you can make a 9-patch block using a combination of squares, half-square triangles, and rectangles. All these are in the Churn Dash block, so refer to Appendix 2 to see what size to cut the pieces. For a 4-patch block, you could combine small squares with half-square triangles, and all the necessary cutting sizes are provided.

Emily, Laetitia, Karis, and Morgan designed their own blocks for their pillows. Emily strip pieced her rectangles, but instead of making the London Stairs pattern, she rearranged them to create a new pattern. Laetitia was going to make a Star, but she cut the center square too small by accident, so she decided to replace it with a 4-patch. When she was about to add the star points, she tried rotating the rectangular Flying Geese units and liked the new pattern better. Karis made 16 half-square tri-

angles and had fun arranging them in several different ways before deciding on her final pattern. Morgan made her block from two half-square triangle units and two squares. Then she set the block on point and added the corners of horse fabric. She also added an embellishment of a horse button in the middle. These kids were new to patchwork and were very excited about making their own unique patterns. They recorded all their work in notebooks and drew diagrams of their quilt blocks to help them see which fabrics went where, and how to lay out the units of the block once they were pieced.

Emily, Laetitia, Karis, and Annie (holding Morgan's pillow) display the pillows they designed.

Crazy Patchwork

Crazy Patchwork blocks are made from irregularly shaped pieces. They are a great way to use up your leftover scraps from other projects. The pillow and the little quilt in this book both use 5½" Crazy Patchwork blocks, but you can make them any size you like. See page 29 for instructions and a picture.

Fusible Appliqué

You can cut out and fuse any shape for appliqué projects. Templates for two sizes of hearts may be found in Appendix 3. Use the large heart for an 8" or 9" block, and use the small one for the 6" squares in the 12" Double 4-patch with Hearts block, or the Ohio Star with Hearts on pages 84 and 97. See page 43 for fusible appliqué instructions. You may embellish these appliqué shapes with machine embroidery.

Lily used her hand as a template to make her block. Then she transformed the fused hand into a chicken by using fabric markers to add the feet, beak, comb, and eye. This is a simple, fun project, especially for younger children. For more chickens made in this way, see the wall hangings, page 70.

This is a wide selection of blocks from which to choose. Enjoy experimenting and don't be afraid to try out your own patterns.

Large Heart and Double 4-patch with Hearts pillows.

Chicken pillow.

Patchwork Pillows, Pillowcases, and Tote Bags

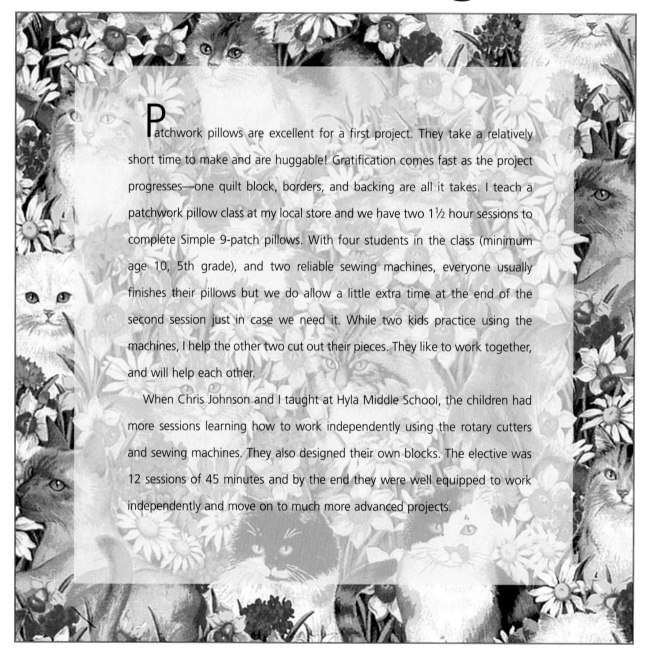

Patchwork pillows are excellent for a first project. They take a relatively short time to make and are huggable! Gratification comes fast as the project progresses—one quilt block, borders, and backing are all it takes. I teach a patchwork pillow class at my local store and we have two 1½ hour sessions to complete Simple 9-patch pillows. With four students in the class (minimum age 10, 5th grade), and two reliable sewing machines, everyone usually finishes their pillows but we do allow a little extra time at the end of the second session just in case we need it. While two kids practice using the machines, I help the other two cut out their pieces. They like to work together, and will help each other.

When Chris Johnson and I taught at Hyla Middle School, the children had more sessions learning how to work independently using the rotary cutters and sewing machines. They also designed their own blocks. The elective was 12 sessions of 45 minutes and by the end they were well equipped to work independently and move on to much more advanced projects.

Patchwork Pillow Patterns

Basic patterns are provided for three different sizes of pillows: 12" x 16", 14" x 14", and 18" x 18".

Use 9" blocks for 12" x 16" and 14" x 14" pillows.

Use 12" blocks for 18" x 18" pillows.

Refer to Appendices 1 and 2 for block patterns and cutting instructions.

Refer to Appendices 1 and 2 for block patterns and cutting instructions.

supplies

- ¾ yd. of fabric for the pillow back and borders
- Assorted small pieces for the patchwork block
- Pillow form

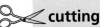

cutting

for 12" x 16" Pillow

Patchwork block:
- (1) 9" (unfinished size 9½")

Borders:
- (2) 2¼" x 9½" top and bottom (add first)
- (2) 4½" x 13" sides

Pillow back:
- (2) 11½" x 13"

for 14" x 14" Pillow:

Patchwork block:
- (1) 9" (unfinished size 9½")

Borders:
- (2) 3¼" x 9½" sides (add first)
- (2) 3¼" x 15" top and bottom

Pillow back:
- (2) 11" x 15"

for 18" x 18" Pillow:

Patchwork block:
- (1) 12" (unfinished size 12½")

Borders:
- (2) 3¾" x 12½" sides (add first)
- (2) 3¾" x 19" top and bottom

Pillow back:
(2) 12½" x 19"

instructions

Adjust the border sizes if you wish to add an additional frame, or if you decide to make a different block size. Refer to Patchwork Blocks, page 49, for several examples of pillows. Cut frames and borders across the full width (42") of fabric. See page 15 for instructions on rotary cutting. For the pillow back, cut a wide strip across the full width of the fabric; for example, 11½" wide, then counter-cut to make two pieces 13" x 11½", for the 12" x 16" pillow. Since these are large, use a 15" square ruler, or the grid on the cutting mat to measure the correct size.

First piece the patchwork block, make a fusible appliqué block, illustrate a block, or use a pre-printed panel. The pre-printed panel is the simplest option.

You can illustrate your blocks with drawings in colored fabric markers. Lisa and Jacqueline made their pil-

Pillows illustrated with fabric markers, 14" x 14" and 12" x 16".

Pre-printed animal block pillow, 18" x 18".

Ramona laying pillow backing on top for stitching.

lows in this way. They drew on 8" blocks and added a 1" frame (cut 1½") to make 9" blocks before adding the border strips.

Siblings Harry, Lily, and Holly each used different methods for their blocks. Harry (age 7) illustrated his block with drawings of diamonds in fabric marker, and Lily (age 10) made a chicken from fusible appliqué. Holly (age 11) pieced four half-square triangle units and arranged them into her favorite pattern.

Once the block is complete, add the borders to finish the pillow top.

Make the pillow back from two overlapping pieces, envelope style, with no snaps, buttons, or zippers. Fold the middle edge of each back piece over by ¼" toward the wrong side and press. Repeat so that you make a hem, tucking the raw edge inside. Machine sew the folds in place using thread that matches the fabric. Lay the pillow top right side up on the table, and lay the backing pieces over it, right sides down so that they overlap with the hemmed folds in the middle. The backing pieces should overlap in the middle by at least 2½". Align all the outer raw edges of the pillow cover.

Alicen stuffs pillow case with pillow form.

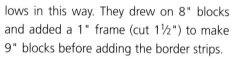

Place right sides of pillow front and backs together. Clip corners before turning right sides out.

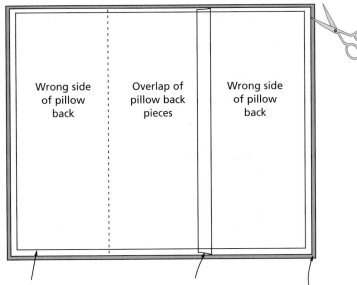

| Wrong side of pillow back | Overlap of pillow back pieces | Wrong side of pillow back |

Stitching line - stitch both back pieces to the front at once.

Fold over the raw edge of the pillow back twice and stitch by machine before attaching to the pillow front.

Pillow front on bottom

Pin the backing and top together. Change to a regular machine foot, and stitch around the edge with a ⅜" seam allowance. When you reach a corner, stop sewing with the needle down ⅜" from the raw edges, raise the presser foot, and turn the corner. Drop the presser foot and continue in the same way until you have sewn all the way around. Sew five or six stitches beyond the starting point so that your stitches overlap. Clip diagonally across the corner seam allowances so that the corners will turn right-side-out.

Turn the pillow cover right-side-out, and stuff in the pillow form. You're done! Toss the pillow in the air and celebrate!

Hyla kids with pillows.

Holly, Lily, and Harry show their pillows.

Hyla kids with pillows.

Donna and Laetitia.

Crazy Patchwork Pillow

For this pillow, you will need four 5½" Crazy Patchwork blocks (6" unfinished size; see instructions on page 29). This is a fun way to use up odd scraps. The pillow has 1" black sashing strips and a 2" border.

instructions

Lay out the Crazy Patchwork blocks into the desired configuration. Join them in rows with the 6" sashing strips in between. Join the rows with the 12½" sashing strips between and along the top and bottom edges. The 14½" strips go on each side. Add the borders just as you would for the other pillows with the shorter strips adjacent to the sides and the longer strips on the top and bottom edges. Complete the back as already directed.

cutting

Sashing:
- (2) 6" x 1½"
- (3) 12½" x 1½"
- (2) 14½" x 1½"

Border:
- (2) 14½" x 2¾" sides
- (2) 19" x 2¾" top and bottom

Pillow back:
- (2) 12½" x 19"

Crazy Patchwork pillow, 18" x 18".

Uncle Sam's Pillow

My daughter, Hazel (age 18), designed and made this pillow a couple of weeks after the tragic events of September 11, 2001. Her task was to make a pillow for a special exhibition sponsored by David Textiles, Inc., "Quilts for the Young at Heart," at Houston International Quilt Market and Festival. She had a variety of David Textiles' fabrics from which to choose, and her idea of using the teddy bears in the flag worked beautifully. She sketched the pattern out on graph paper and calculated all the cutting sizes perfectly. Being computer literate, it took her no time at all to program the sewing machine to embroider "September 11 2001, In Remembrance" on the red strips. I was very touched by her creativity, as were many at the Houston Festival.

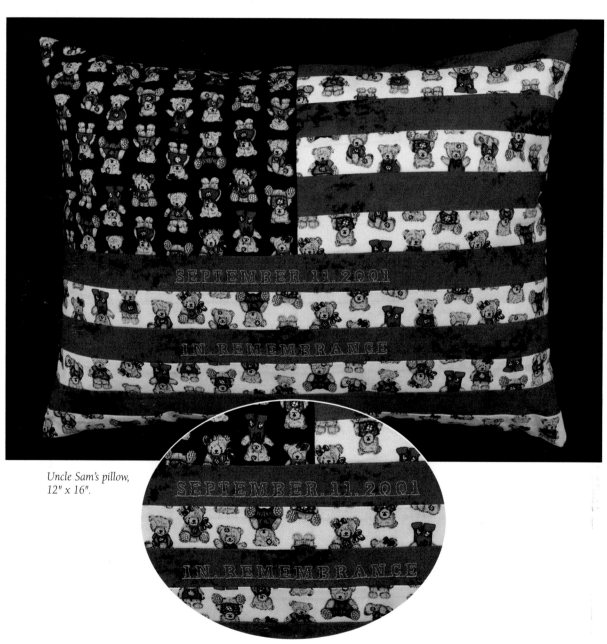

Uncle Sam's pillow,
12" x 16".

cutting

Note: ½" seam allowance is included for the pillow edge.

Blue:
- (1) 6¾" x 8¾"
- (2) 11½" x 13" (pillow back)

Red:
- (3) 1½" x 17"
- (2) 1½" x 8¾"
- (1) 1¾" x 8¾"

White:
- (2) 1½" x 17"
- (1) 1¾" x 17"
- (3) 1½" x 8¾"

supplies

- ½ yd. blue for blue corner rectangle and pillow back
- ¼ yd. each of red and white fabric
- 12" x 16" pillow form

instructions

Join the strips together, paying attention to the placement of the ones that are wider; these have the additional seam allowance for the outer edge of the pillow, so place them adjacent to the outer edge. Join the red and white 17" strips together alternately with the wide white strip (1¾" x 17") on the bottom edge. Likewise, join the 8¾" strips, making sure that the 1¾" wide white one is on the top edge. Once the short strips are in one piece, attach them to the short edge of the blue rectangle. Next, sew the two sections (one made from short strips and a rectangle, and the other from long strips) of the block together to complete the flag. Complete the back as already directed.

Bed Pillowcases

Colorful bed pillowcases are not difficult to make and will add a cheerful note to the bedroom. They also make great gifts. There is a wonderful selection of printed cottons from which to choose. Theme prints, such as the soccer and cat fabrics shown, are fun to use.

The pattern uses three different fabrics and the pillowcase fits a standard sized bed pillow. The narrow strip between the body of the pillowcase and the open hemmed end provides an attractive accent. A bright solid color is often a good choice to offset the print in the body of the pillowcase.

✂ cutting

Body:
- (1) 41" x 27"

Hem:
- (1) 41" x 9"

Trim:
- (1) 1½" x 41"

supplies

- ¾ yd. body of pillowcase
- ¼ yd. hem
- ⅛ yd. trim

To make two matching pillowcases, double the amounts for the body and hem; ⅛ yard of trim is enough for two.

instructions

Press the trim in half lengthwise with the wrong sides together. Sandwich the trim between the hem and the pillow body, right sides together. You should have four raw edges to sew. Use a ¼" seam allowance. Sew, and then press the seam allowance toward the hem. The trim lies toward the pillow body. Press the hem edge ½" under to the wrong side, and then press the hem in half so that it will encase the seam with the body of the pillowcase and trim. Open out these folds to join the side seams of the pillowcase. Use French seams to sew the sides and bottom. See page 29 for instructions on French seams.

Refold the hem end folds and stitch them so that they encase the seam joining the hem to the main body. To do this, top stitch on the right side of the pillowcase on the trim, in the ditch (as close to the seam of the hem as possible). Use thread that matches the trim. Pin carefully and frequently to make sure that you stitch through the hem on the inside of the pillow case and enclose all the raw edges of the trim seam. This is the most challenging part of making the pillowcase. Machine stitching over all the layers where the side seams come together may be a little tough. If you have trouble, simply hand stitch that small section.

Flannel pillowcases are very soft and kids love them. If you decide to use flannel, use it for the pillow body and hem, but stick to regular cotton for the trim since it will be less bulky and easier to sew. Some prints are available in both flannel and regular cotton so you can coordinate quilts and pillowcases, like the example shown below. For the Rail Fence quilt pattern, see page 111.

Rail Fence quilt with matching flannel pillow.

Tote Bags

Tote bags are not only fun to make, but they are useful! You can make the bag from one or two fabrics, or jazz it up by adding a patchwork block to the front.

Holly and Lily with their tote bags.

cutting for the bag

Body of the bag:
- (1) 17" x 30"

Straps:
- (2) 3¾" x 33"

Frame for block:
- 1 full-width 2" strip cut into (2) 9½" and (2) 11" strips.

supplies

- ½ yd. body of the bag
- ¼ yd. bag handles
- 9" patchwork block to embellish the bag and frame (optional)
- ⅛ yd. frame to attach the patchwork block to the bag

instructions

Making a Frame for the Block

Fold the 9½" strips in half lengthwise with the right sides out and press. Attach the raw edges to the sides of the blocks. Press with the seams toward the frame. Turn each end of the 11" strips in by ¼" toward the wrong side and press. Fold in half lengthwise and press. Attach these strips to the top and bottom edges of the block. Make them fit exactly and backstitch at the beginning and end of the seams. Press the seams toward the frame. Now you have a block with a frame, with folds on the sides and no raw edges, which can be appliquéd onto the body of the bag. Position the block with frame on the tote bag piece (17" x 30"), 2¾" from one of the 17" sides and 1¾" from the bottom edge. Pin it in place and sew around the edge, with either a straight stitch or a zigzag stitch, as close to the edge of the frame as possible. Use thread that matches the frame, or pick a contrasting color to make it more decorative.

Assembling the Bag

Press a ¼"-⅜" fold toward the wrong side on each of the long edges of the straps, and then iron them in half lengthwise with the right sides out. Sew a straight stitch or a zigzag ⅛" from each edge of the straps, sewing the edge with the seam allowance folds first.

On the bag top, fold over ½" to the wrong side and press, and then fold again 1½" and press to make the hem fold. Unfold to join the bag sides. Sew the bag sides using a French seam. See page 29 for instructions on French seams.

Insert and pin the strap ends under the hem fold 3" from each side of the bag. One strap goes on the front side of the bag and the other on the back. Make sure that the straps are not twisted. Pin and stitch down the 1½" hem, using a straight stitch, in thread that matches the bag body. Add additional stitching where the straps are tucked into the hem so that they are really strong—stitch a square, and then diagonal lines in an X across the square.

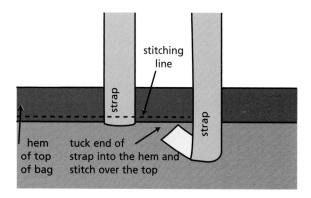

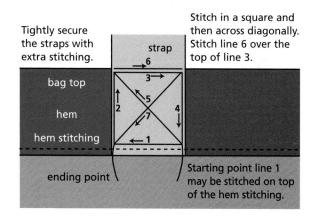

Finally, stitch the bottom of the bag with a French seam. For the second seam, start and end with three or four backstitches. Well done! Your bag is finished.

Wall Hangings

Bear Quilt, machine quilted, 34" x 41".

Small quilts can make decorative wall hangings to brighten up your home, and make excellent gifts. The wall hangings illustrated are more for inspiration than for duplicating, although I've included a couple of the patterns. The simplest idea is to take a preprinted panel and add a patchwork border. Also, there are all sorts of techniques for making fabric art that can be incorporated into quilts. Those shown on the following pages include fusible appliqué, drawing on fabric with fabric markers and using rubber stamps, machine embroidery, and transferring images from a computer onto fabric. For more ideas, refer to my first book *Creative Quilting with Kids* (Krause Publications, 2001). Cindy Walter's book *Snippet Sensations* (Krause Publications, 1999) is a great guide for pictorial fusible appliqué. See page 42 for instructions to make quilt hangers.

Preprinted Panel

I couldn't resist this bear panel shown on the preceding page, and when I took the quilt to school to show the kids, they just loved it. Use any sized panel and add a border. This bear panel is 24" x 32" so I was easily able to divide the sides evenly to make the patchwork border. Each rectangle is 4" x 2" (cut 4½" x 2½") so there are eight along the top and bottom edges and six along the sides, with 2" squares in the corners. Then I added an outer border with cornerstones to complete the quilt top. You can make the borders as simple or as complex as you like. One frame with or without cornerstones may be all you want, or you can add multiple frames and/or have piecing within the frame as I did with the rectangles. You could even make small four patch units joined into a checkered border. There are plenty of possibilities. I kept the quilting simple, outlining the bear and the other animals and using a serpentine stitch in the borders.

Fusible Appliqué

You can make wonderful pictures from a wide assortment of fabrics with fusible appliqué. See page 43 for instructions.

Jacqueline (age 9) made an underwater scene and cut out several different tropical fish from my stash of fish fabric to fuse. She had fun arranging the rocks and weeds, and it was her idea to have some of the fish swimming behind the weeds to add a 3-D quality to the picture. She began with a background of 16" x 22". After she had completed the fusing, we trimmed it a little to make sure it was absolutely square before adding the 2½" borders.

Jacqueline's Coral Reef, machine quilted, 20" x 25".

Lisa (age 11) made the beautiful butterfly. She began by drawing the butterfly on blank newsprint so that she had a pattern to use when cutting out the pieces of fabric to fuse. Her background was 17" x 22". After fusing, Lisa machine embroidered in blanket stitch around all the edges of the fused pieces in a variety of colors including some glossy and gold thread. This adds an extra sparkle to her wall hanging and it is most attractive. She also added a 2½" border.

Lisa and Jacqueline both made their quilts envelope style, laying down the batting, and then the backing and front right sides together. They stitched all the way around except for about 6", and turned the quilts right sides out. The opening was hand stitched closed, so no binding was required. They both stitched in the ditch next to the border. Jacqueline quilted with a serpentine stitch that looks like waves, and Lisa outline-quilted her butterfly. They also attached loops to the top edges of the quilts to hang them.

Lisa's Butterfly, machine embroidered and quilted, 21½" x 26".

Sophie (age 11) made a family of chickens using drawings of her family members' hands. Her Dad is the biggest, facing the other three—her Mom, herself, and her little sister. She used fabric markers to add beaks, combs, eyes, and feet to the chickens. Then, she hand embroidered and machine embroidered around the chickens.

Like the fish and the butterfly, this is a large central panel with borders. Sophie appliquéd the chickens onto a background measuring approximately 15" x 28", and then added 1¼" and 3" borders. Sophie did free-motion machine quilting around the chickens and a serpentine stitch in the border. She machine stitched the binding to the back of the quilt, then brought it to the front and secured it with a zigzag machine stitch.

9-Patch Chickens

Sophie helped me make this machine-quilted wall hanging. She made the chicken blocks for me using her hand outlines and her sister's—a delightful way to display the blocks, and to take advantage of some of the wonderful chicken theme fabrics that are available.

Sophie with Spring Chickens wall hanging.

9-patch Chickens, machine quilted, 35½" x 35½".

cutting

Pale background fabric:
- (4) 9" squares

Chicken theme fabric:
- (5) 9" squares

Fabric for hands:
- (4) 7" squares backed with
  Steam-a-Seam 2

Dark inner border:
- (2) 1¾" x 26" sides
- (2) 1¾" x 28½" top and bottom

Chicken outer border:
- (2) 4" x 28½" sides
- (2) 4" x 35½" top and bottom

supplies

- ⅓ yd. pale background for the hands
- 7" squares of a variety of fabrics for the four hands
- 28" Steam-a-Seam 2 to fuse hands
- (5) 9" squares chicken theme fabric (you may use any combination of fabrics. I used 4 of 1 fabric and a different one for the center square)
- ¼ yd. dark fabric for the inner border
- 1¼ yd. chicken fabric for the outer border (cut the side strips down the length of the fabric so that the chickens are the right way up. If the fabric has chickens going in all directions, or the direction of the pattern does not matter, ½ yd. is sufficient.)
- Fabric markers to draw the beaks, eyes, combs, and feet onto the chickens
- ⅓ yd. fabric for binding
- 40" x 40" batting
- 1¼ yd. backing

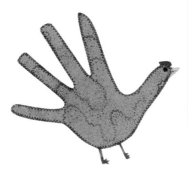

instructions

Trace the hands onto the paper on the back of the squares with Steam-a-Seam 2, and then cut them out carefully. A few pins will help to stop the paper from shifting while you are cutting. Fuse the hands onto the background and use fabric markers to add beaks, feet, combs, and eyes to make them into chickens. If you want to hand embroider around the chickens, do this before you join the blocks. Make the 9-patch by joining the squares of chicken hands and commercial chicken fabric into rows, and then joining the rows. Add the inner dark border sewing the two shorter pieces onto the sides and the longer ones onto the top and bottom. Do the same for the outer chicken border.

For an attractive outline around the chickens, sew with a zigzag or blanket stitch through the edge of the fused pieces. I quilted with a serpentine stitch along the seam lines and in the border strips. The rest of the quilting was free-motion. I did an echo line around the fused chickens and followed the outlines of the chickens on the commercial prints. Another option would be a simple meander stitch in the blocks. Enjoy those chickens!

Machine Embroidered Hearts

Sophie (age 11) made this gorgeous, little wall hanging and gave it to her parents for Christmas. Needless to say, they were thrilled with it. She had great fun machine embroidering the fused hearts, and loved trying out the different stitches in fancy threads.

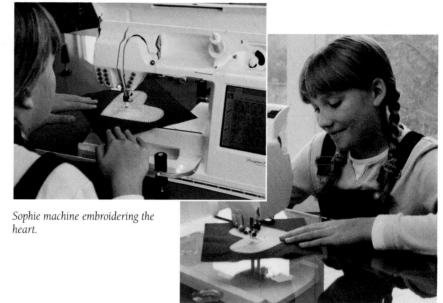

Sophie machine embroidering the heart.

From Sophie with Love, machine embroidered and quilted, 24" x 24".

✂ cutting

Blocks:
- (4) 8½" squares

Center square:
- (1) 2½" square

Hearts:
- (4) 7" squares backed with Steam-a-Seam 2
- (1) 2" square for the center heart, backed with Steam-a-Seam 2 (optional)

Sashing:
- (4) 2½" x 8½"

Inner border:
- (2) 1½" x 18½" sides
- (2) 1½" x 20½" top and bottom

Outer border:
- (2) 2½" x 20½" sides
- (2) 2½" x 24½" top and bottom

supplies

- ¼ yd. background for blocks
- ¼ yd. contrasting fabric for hearts (Sophie did 2 in pale purple and 2 in pink)
- ¼ yd. sashing and inner border
- ⅓ yd. outer border
- 28" Steam-a-Seam 2 to fuse hearts
- 27" x 27" batting
- ¾ yd. backing

instructions

Use the large heart in Appendix 3. You can trace it onto the paper from the Steam-a-Seam 2, or onto cardboard to make a template. The center small heart is optional (no pattern provided). Cut out the hearts and fuse them into the center of the blocks. See page 43 for more detailed instructions on fusible appliqué. Next, machine embroider the hearts (instructions on page 20). Sulky has a huge variety of fancy threads and the kids love to use them and experiment with different stitches. Don't forget to change your needle to a Size 90 Topstitch when you use the metallic threads.

Once the hearts are completed, join the blocks to the sashing strips in rows and then join the rows together. Add the narrow inner border, sewing the shorter strips to the sides first, and then the longer strips to the top and bottom edges. Repeat for the outer border. The quilt was made envelope style, so no binding was needed—see instructions for the Coral Reef and Butterfly quilts (pages 67 and 68). Sophie used the serpentine stitch to quilt along the seam lines, and she quilted around each heart. She added an extra line of quilting in the border about ½" from the edge of the quilt. Sophie made loops to hang her quilt. Alternatively, you can attach a hanging sleeve (see page 42 for instructions).

Illustrations with Fabric Markers and Rubber Stamps

Sophie's Family Quilt, machine quilted, 36" x 36".

Sophie used fabric markers, Fantastix, and rubber stamps with Fabrico stamp pads to illustrate the blocks and decorate the border strips in this delightful wall hanging. See page 44 for instructions. Read and follow the directions carefully for the products you choose.

The blocks illustrated with family members and home are made from unbleached muslin squares, 15" in the center and 8" in the corners. Dark solid color 1" frames around the blocks make them stand out clearly so that the pictures are well displayed. The 3" pale yellow strips in the border have rubber stamped images and each one represents a season of the year. Sophie machine quilted with serpentine and straight line stitching. In the center block she free-motion machine quilted and even stitched in her name.

Sophie with her quilt.

Computer Images on Fabric

Family Pets, machine quilted, 20" x 21".

Our family pets star in this little wall hanging. My daughter, Hazel, e-mailed me the photographs and I printed them from the computer onto ColorPlus fabric using an ink jet printer. In the spotlight are Snowy the bunny, Pelé the cat sleeping and playing, George the horse, and Hazel riding George.

Black frames were added to the pictures, and then trimmed so that they would fit together. After auditioning numerous fabrics for the border, I found that this bright one perked up all the colors in the pictures. Several dark fabrics I tried made the photos look dull.

The serpentine quilting stitch in the variegated chartreuse thread shows up nicely on the black sashing. The big horse picture is a fairly large area without quilting, but since the quilt will hang on the wall and not receive much wear and tear, it should be fine. You can use any photographs. A little quilt like this with family photos would make a wonderful gift for grandparents. The quilt can be any size with just one or many pictures. It is easiest to piece pictures that are all the same size. Be imaginative! You can even combine photographs with pieced blocks or appliqué.

Little Quilts and Receiving Blankets

These quilts are just right for dolls and stuffed animals, and the blankets are the perfect size for premature babies, or you can make them into wall hangings. We used several techniques, including quilts with and without binding, machine and hand quilted quilts, tied quilts, and flannel backed blankets with no batting or binding. You may select whichever method suits you the best. In choosing, consider the use for the quilt, and how much time you have to make it. The least time consuming quilts are those made envelope style without binding, and tied, but these are not quite as robust as the quilted and bound ones. The preemie baby receiving blankets are less complicated than the quilts, as they have no batting and are envelope-style without binding. Since they consist of only two layers, the top and the flannel backing can be top stitched together without changing the foot or the settings on the machine. The flannel makes a beautifully soft backing for the blanket and the kids love it. The preemie babies and their parents appreciate it too!

supplies

Since all the quilts are alike in size, the fabric requirements are similar. For this reason, I have not listed the supplies for each individual quilt. Simply use the following list as a guide, omitting those items that are not relevant to your particular quilt or receiving blanket (for example, binding fabric or batting).

- ¼ yd. pieces or smaller in a selection of fabrics for the quilt top
- Steam-a-Seam 2 for projects with fused hearts
- ⅓ yd. borders
- ¼ yd. binding
- 27" x 27" batting
- ¾ yd. regular cotton or flannel for backing

Little quilts or receiving blankets, ranging in size from 20" to 26" along the sides, are ideal beginning quilting projects. There are all sorts of possibilities, from the very simple strippy quilts and 25-square grids to the more challenging enlarged Bear Paw block with lots of triangles. I hope the many quilts illustrated will inspire you, and that you will have fun designing your own variations on the patterns. There are some repeated patterns, but each uses differing fabrics or layout. You will soon find that you can make a huge variety of quilts from one simple pattern, just by changing the block orientation or the position of the dark and light fabrics. I have provided some blank grids in the Appendices for you to photocopy and color, and encourage you to explore different options on paper before cutting up your fabric.

At Hyla Middle School, the kids made preemie baby blankets to donate to the University of Washington Hospital Neonatal Intensive Care Unit. They were delighted to participate in this outreach program and took great pride in designing and sewing the blankets for the babies.

Hyla kids show their preemie baby blankets.

general instructions

The cutting instructions given for each project refer only to the quilt top. Plan your quilt before you start cutting the fabrics. I recommend making an annotated sketch so that you know exactly which fabrics go where in the pattern. Write down the sizes of the shapes, and the number of pieces you need to cut for each fabric. It is so easy to lose track of the pieces. If you have it written down, you can be systematic and check as you cut. This saves time and errors, and helps you remember where you are, especially if you are interrupted in the middle, or run out of time.

Emily and Sarah wrap the animals.

Plan your piecing so that you always sew in straight lines and never have to inset seams. Usually this involves piecing any subdivided squares first, then joining all the square units into rows. In tops made from four or more quilt blocks, make all the blocks and then join them in rows, including sashing if you have any. You can then sew the rows together. I often use small sticky labels to number my pieces, which helps me sew them in the correct order and assembly line piece efficiently.

When you reach the borders, most of them are cut either 2½" or 3" wide. If you cut three strips across the full width of the fabric, you should be able to get the two short side borders out of one strip (unless the sides of the center of the top are bigger than 21"), and the top and bottom borders from the other two strips. Therefore, for almost all the quilts, ¼ yard

should be enough for the borders. If, before adding the border, the sides are greater than 21", or your fabric is less than 42" wide, you will need to cut four strips, which will use ⅓ yard. The cutting measurements provided for border strips assume consistent ¼" seam allowances in the pieced center. If your seam allowances are inaccurate, the border strips will not fit exactly. Piece and measure the central area before you cut the border strips, so that you can adjust the lengths of the border strips if necessary.

The quilts are divided up according to the piecing techniques used, starting with the simplest and progressing to more challenging projects. Remember that you can adapt these patterns in any way, combining different blocks, designing your own patterns, and adding extra borders, etc.

Laurel, Donna, and Laetitia pamper the stuffed animals.

Refer to Section One for more detailed technical instructions:

Quilts Made from Simple Piecing

Simple piecing is the joining of single square or rectangular pieces together. There are no triangles or strip piecing. For instructions on machine piecing the patchwork, refer to Section One, page 21.

The Strippy and Split Strippy Quilts

The simplest quilt is a Strippy, made from seven strips sewn together, with borders added. In the example shown, made with snowflake fabric, the three layers were joined envelope style and the quilt was tied.

Snowflake Strippy quilt, envelope style and tied, 26" x 22½".

✂ cutting

(see page 77 for supplies)

Dark strips:
- (4) 3" x 18½" (from 2 full-width strips)

Light strips:
- (3) 3" x 18½" (from 2 full-width strips)

Dark inner top and bottom borders:
- (2) 2" x 18" (from one full-width strip)

Outer pale borders:
- (2) 3" x 21½" sides
- (2) 3" x 23" top and bottom

Split Strippy preemie baby blanket, 26" x 22½".

✂ cutting

(see page 77 for supplies)

Dark strips:
- (7) 3" x 11¾" (from 3 full-width strips)

Light strips:
- (7) 3" x 7¼" (from 2 full-width strips)

Pale inner top and bottom borders:
- (2) 2" x 18" (from 1 full-width strip)

Outer border:
- (2) 3" x 21½" sides
- (2) 3" x 23" top and bottom

The Split Strippy design is the same layout as the simple Strippy, except that each strip is split, and by alternating the direction the strips lie, a new pattern is created. Join the two fabrics to create the seven strips and then proceed as for the simple Strippy. This little pansy Split Strippy is a preemie baby blanket with floral flannel backing.

Assorted 25-Patch Quilts

This very simple pattern has many possibilities. The quilts consist of (25) 4" squares in a 5 x 5 format, with borders added. The five examples illustrated clearly demonstrate a wide variety from the same basic pattern.

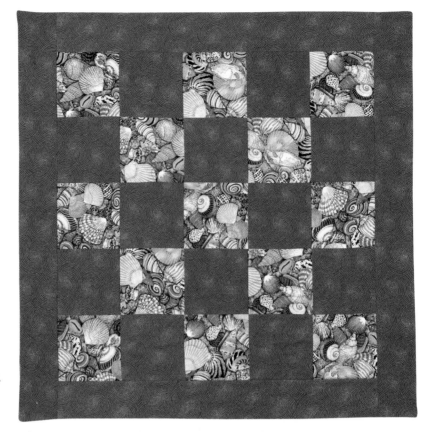

Checkerboard preemie baby blanket, 25" x 25".

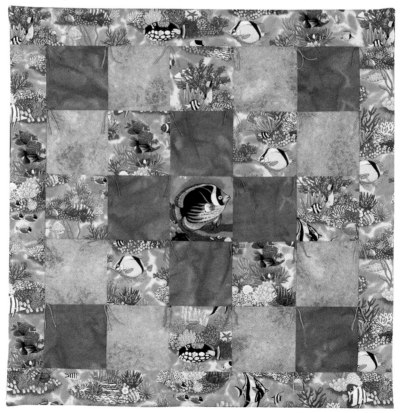

Trip around the World Fish Quilt, envelope style and tied, 25" x 25".

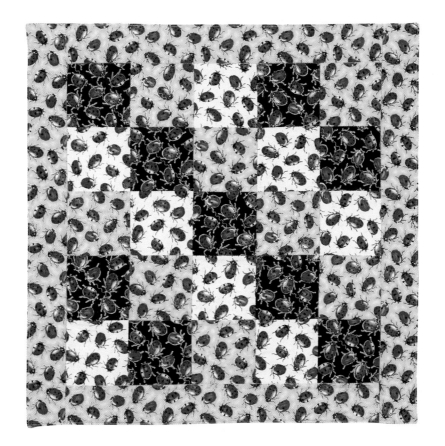

Diagonal Ladybugs preemie baby blanket, 25" x 25".

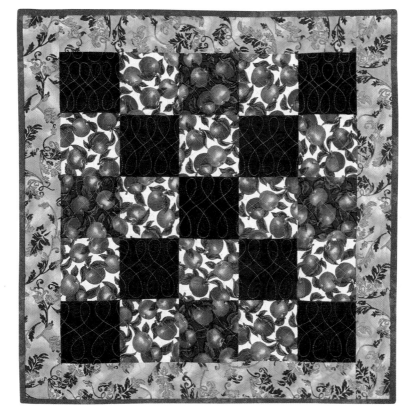

X Quilt, commercially quilted, 25" x 25".

Scrappy Quilt with every square different, machine quilted, 25" x 25".

Plan the pattern so you know how many squares of each color to cut. You can use the patterns shown in the photographs as a guide, (just count the number of squares of each color), or design your own. Photocopy Appendix 6, the 25 square grid, and color in the squares, or simply cut out a variety of 4½" fabric squares and play with them. You may like to fussy-cut particular motifs to appear in the squares. The fish, in the example shown above, were fussy-cut. Make a quick sketch of the pattern and count up the number of squares of each color so you know how many to cut.

Griffen, Emelie, and Miles with their 25-patch preemie baby blankets.

Strip Piecing

Strip piecing is a time saving technique in which strips of fabric are sewn together, and then counter-cut into pieced sections. Hence, when making, for example, multiple 4-patch units, you do not need to cut out every individual square. For detailed instructions, see Section One, page 25. Here are the patterns for five quilts using strip piecing. The two 4-patch, and the Double 9-patch quilts are made from strip pieced squares, while the London Stairs and Strippy Triad utilize rectangles.

4-Patch Quilts

Eight 4-patch units, alternated with large squares, make up the 4-patch and Squares preemie blanket. You may fussy-cut the large squares. Grace cut squares of farm animals to go between her 4-patches.

Grace with her 4-patch and Squares preemie baby blanket.

4-patch and Squares preemie baby blanket, 25" x 25"

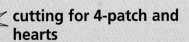

cutting for 4-patch and squares

(see page 77 for supplies)

4-patches:

- 2 full-width 3" strips of each fabric. Piece the strips and counter-cut (16) 3"

Alternating squares:

- (8) 5½" squares (fussy-cut if desired)

Borders:

- (2) 3" x 20½" sides
- (2) 3" x 25½" top and bottom

cutting for 4-patch and hearts

(see page 77 for supplies)

4-patches:

- 1 full-width 3½" strip of each fabric. Piece the strips and counter-cut (10) 3½".

Background for hearts:

- (4) 6½" squares

Hearts:

- (4) 5" squares backed with Steam-a-Seam 2

Borders:

- (2) 3½" x 18½" sides
- (2) 3½" x 24½" top and bottom

Christmas 4-patch and Hearts quilt, machine quilted, 24" x 24".

instructions

I enlarged the pattern slightly and added fused hearts to the big squares. In this quilt, there are only five 4-patch units, and four squares with hearts. See page 43 for instructions for fusible appliqué, and Appendix 3 for the small heart template. You may blanket stitch by hand, or machine embroider around the hearts.

For both these quilts, first strip piece the 4-patch units, and then join them in rows alternating with the big squares. Assemble the rows and add the borders.

Double 9-Patch Quilt

The Double 9-patch is so called because there are small 9-patches within the 9-patch grid. It is made from five small squared 9-patches alternating with four large squares. The large squares provide an opportunity to use pictorial or theme fabrics that you can fussy-cut, like the example shown. When scouring my fabric stash to find a suitable dark fabric for the small 9-patches to go with the cat squares, the best one was the feather fabric. Later, I thought this was perhaps a little macabre—fat and happy cats lounging around after their meal of birds! People seem to either love or hate this little quilt.

✂ cutting for double 9-patch
(see page 77 for supplies)

Dark fabric for 9-patches:
- 3 full-width 2¾" strips

Light fabric for 9-patches:
- 2 full-width 2¾" strips

Large squares:
- (4) 7¼" squares (fussy-cut if desired)

Borders:
- (2) 3" x 20¾" sides
- (2) 3" x 25¾" top and bottom

Kitty 9-Patch quilt, machine quilted, 25½" x 25½".

instructions

To make the 9-patch units, cut one light strip and one dark strip in half. Use these short pieces to make the center set of small squares (pieced in a sequence of light, dark, light). Counter-cut the strips to make five 2¾" strips of squares. Use the long strips to piece the other sequence—dark, light, dark. Counter-cut this set to make (10) 2¾" strips of squares. Join the strips of squares to create the 9-patches and then assemble them with the big squares. Proceed as for the 4-patch. I quilted my cat blocks with a free-motion meander and used the walking foot for the serpentine stitching along the edges and diagonals of the 9-patches. The binding was machine stitched to the back and then brought forward and attached to the front with a zigzag stitch.

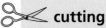

London Stairs

London Stairs is a simple strip pieced pattern made from two contrasting fabrics.

 **cutting**

(see page 77 for supplies)

Two fabrics:
- 3 full-width 2½" strips of each

Borders:
- (2) 3" x 20½" sides
- (2) 3" x 25½" top and bottom

London Stairs preemie baby blanket, 25" x 25".

instructions

Join the strips in pairs, one of each color. Press the seams toward the darker fabric and counter-cut (25) 4½" squares. Arrange these in a grid of 5 x 5 alternating the direction of the rectangles. Use the photograph as a guide. You should have a zigzag that travels all the way from a top corner to the diagonal bottom corner. Join all these square units in rows, and then assemble the rows and add the borders. It may help to number the squares with small sticky labels so that you sew them in the correct order and orientation. Feel free to make different patterns from these square units—it's fun to play and create your own design.

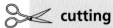

Strippy Triad

This pattern involves sewing three wide strips together and counter-cutting to obtain rows of three rectangles joined on their short sides.

✂ **cutting**

(see page 77 for supplies)

Two fabrics:
- 1 full-width 6" strip of each

Borders:
- (2) 3" x 18" sides
- (2) 3" x 22" top and bottom

Strippy Triad preemie baby blanket, 22½ x 21½.

instructions

Divide the full-width strips into three, so that you have a total of six strips—three of Fabric A and three of Fabric B—each about 14" long. Join along the 14" edges in one sequence of ABA, and the other sequence of BAB. Press the seams toward the darker fabric. Counter-cut these wide pieces into 3" strips of three rectangles. Cut four of ABA and three of BAB. Assemble the quilt top by joining these rows alternately, and then adding the borders. This is not nearly as complicated as it sounds. Give it a go!

Piecing with Corner Triangles

Corner triangles are constructed by cutting squares and sewing diagonally from corner to corner to create triangles. The beauty of them is that you don't have to cut out individual triangles and sew bias edges. For instructions on sewing corner triangles, see Section One, page 27. Here are three different patterns using corner triangles: the Bowtie, the Snowball, and a Star.

Red and White Bowties preemie baby quilt—blocks adjacent, colors reversed in two blocks, 24" x 24".

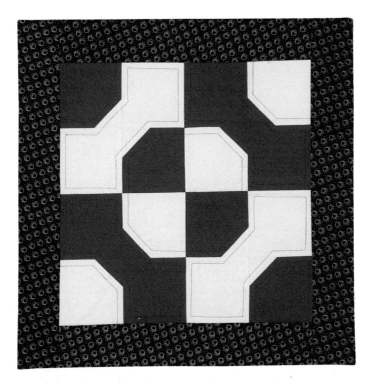

Marbleized Bowties, machine quilted—all blocks oriented in different directions, with colored sashing and cornerstones, 24" x 24".

The Bowtie

The Bowtie quilts demonstrate the variety of designs created by simply changing the orientation of the four blocks, reversing the colors in half of the blocks, or sashing with different colors

instructions

Photocopy and use the grid in Appendix 7 to play with the Bowtie pattern. You can cut out the individual blocks and turn them in different directions, or leave spaces between them to create sashing. As you will see, there are many possibilities.

Draw a sketch of your quilt pattern and itemize the components as a guide for cutting the pieces. If you like one of the examples illustrated above, just use the photograph as a guide and simply count the pieces of each color.

cutting
(see page 77 for supplies)

9" Bowtie blocks:
- (16) 5" squares (8 Bowtie fabric, 8 background)
- (8) 2½" squares (Bowtie fabric)

Borders for a quilt with no sashing:
- (2) 3½" x 18½" sides
- (2) 3½" x 24½" top and bottom

Quilt with sashing and cornerstones:
Sashing strips:
- (12) 2½" x 9½"
Cornerstones:
- (9) 2½" squares

Quilt with sashing the same color as the background:
Sashing in background fabric:
- (2) 1½" x 9½" between pairs of blocks
- (1) 1½" x 19½" middle strip between rows of blocks

Inner border in background fabric:
- (2) 1¾" x 19½" sides
- (2) 1¾" x 22" top and bottom

Outer border:
- (2) 3" x 22" sides
- (2) 3" x 27" top and bottom

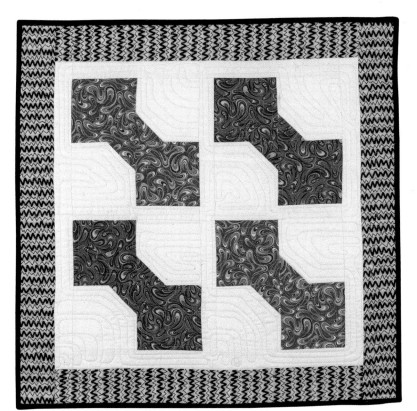

Red and Blue Bowties, commercially quilted—all blocks oriented in the same direction, sashing is the same color as the block background, 26½" x 26½".

Snowball Quilt

Penguin Snowball quilt, tied and beaded, 26½" x 26½".

✂ cutting

(see page 77 for supplies)

Theme fabric and alternating fabric:
- (9) 7½" squares, 5 of one fabric and 4 of the other

Corner triangles:
- (20) 2¾" squares, contrasting the (5) 7½" squares (from 2 full-width strips)
- (16) 2¾" squares, contrasting the (4) 7½" squares (from 2 full-width strips)

Borders:
- (2) 3" x 21½" sides
- (2) 3" x 26½" top and bottom

The Snowball pattern has large squares with corner triangles. These are ideal for theme fabrics. If you place pictorial fabrics in every block, the quilt will probably appear too busy, so I suggest alternating the blocks with a more subdued fabric that differs in value. The penguins show up nicely between the dark snowflake blocks. The corner triangles should also contrast the larger pieces to make them visible, so that they contribute to the pattern. In this quilt, the back was cut 1" larger all around and pressed to the front. I folded it and topstitched in with a zigzag stitch to finish the edge, instead of adding binding. The quilt is tied, except in each penguin block, where a small bead was sewn onto the penguin's eye.

instructions

Piece all the corner triangles first, (see page 27 for instructions). Press the seams toward the dark triangles, and away from the light triangles. When joining the square units, the seams where the triangles meet should butt in opposite directions and lie flat.

Laetitia and Sarah with Snowball preemie baby blankets.

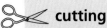

Star Quilt

Kids love this Star pattern, and the corner triangle method (see page 27 for detailed instructions) is an easy way to make accurate points on the stars. For the star points, two corner triangles are joined onto each rectangle of background fabric. To maintain these points, take extra care with pinning when you sew the four star blocks together and add the borders. Note: These rectangular units with triangles are also known as Flying Geese.

instructions

Begin by piecing the corner triangles (star points) onto the background rectangles. Next assemble the three rows that make up the block, i.e. two rows made from two background corner squares and a star points rectangle, and one row made from two star points rectangles and the center square of the star. Finish the blocks by joining these rows. For the outer border, add the corners to two of the strips to make the top and bottom.

✂ cutting

(see page 77 for supplies)

Star centers:
- (4) 5" squares

Star points:
- (32) 2¾" squares

Background fabric:
- (16) 2¾" squares
- (16) 5" x 2¾" rectangles

Inner border:
- (2) 1½" x 18½" sides
- (2) 1½" x 20½" top and bottom

Outer border:
- (4) 3" x 20½" strips
- (4) 3" squares, corners

Star quilt, commercially quilted, 25½" x 25½".

Fast Pieced Half-Square Triangles

Half-square triangle units are fast to piece using the method described in Section One, page 27. Take extra care with your pinning and piecing when you join them, so that you do not lose the triangle points, or have them floating in thin air. This is a little more challenging than the patterns provided so far.

16 Half-Square Triangle Units

This is a great opportunity for you to be creative. With 16 half-square triangle units, there are dozens of ways to arrange them. Each unit has four options for orientation. You can make Pinwheels, Flying Geese, Boxes, symmetrical, or asymmetrical designs. Use the grid in Appendix 8 to photocopy and color. For each unit, make one triangle dark and the other light in value. You can cut out the squares and rearrange them to make different patterns. Alternately, simply piece your fabric 16 half-square triangle units and play with them until you find a pleasing configuration. The two examples here show you some of the pattern possibilities. Another is on a pillow made by Karis, illustrated on page 52.

instructions

Piece the half-square triangle units following the directions in Section One, page 27. They should measure 5" (unfinished). If they are not 5", make sure that they are all the same size before you join them, and adjust the size of the border strips to fit.

Sixteen half-square triangle units all oriented in the same direction, envelope style, and tied, 25½" x 25½".

 **cutting**

(see page 77 for supplies)

Half-square triangle units, light and dark fabrics:

- (16) 5⅜" squares, 8 light and 8 dark. You can use a variety of fabrics. I used unbleached muslin for the light, and assorted darks. (Option: cut the squares slightly larger and then trim the half-square triangle units to exactly 5".)

Inner narrow border:

- (2) 1½" x 18½" sides
- (2) 1½" x 20½" top and bottom

Outer border without cornerstones:

- (2) 3" x 20½" sides
- (2) 3" x 25½" top and bottom

Outer border with cornerstones:

- (4) 3" x 20½" strips
- (4) 3" squares, corners

Sixteen half-square triangle units with a variety of patterns—Pinwheel, Flying Geese, and Boxes, commercially quilted, 25½" x 25½".

Bear Paw

The Bear Paw is the most challenging of the little quilts and probably one of the most difficult projects in this book. Gain some experience making simpler quilts before attempting this one. It is one Bear Paw block enlarged from the traditional block size of between 9" and 12" to 19¼". The half-square triangle units are 3¼" unfinished, so they are manageable and not too small and fiddly. Precise piecing with ¼" seams is vital for accurate assembly. Hence, the half-square triangles are made larger than necessary and then trimmed exactly to 3¼". Such precision was not required for the Bowtie (16 half-square triangles) since, as long as all the units are the same size, they can be joined together accurately. In the Bear Paw, the half-square triangles must be sewn onto other shapes, so their size is much more critical.

✂ cutting

(see page 77 for supplies)

Half-square triangle units, Bear Paw, and background fabrics:
- (8) 4" squares of each

Bear Paw fabric:
- (4) 6" squares
- (1) 3¼" center square

Background sashing strips:
- (4) 3¼" x 8¾"

Border with cornerstones:
- (4) 3½" x 19¾" strips
- (4) 3½" squares, corners

Bear Paw quilt, commercially quilted, 26" x 26".

Begin by piecing the half-square triangles (see Section One, page 27 for instructions). Next, trim them all to exactly 3¼" square, maintaining the triangle points in the corners of the square units. You will probably have to trim a little off all four sides to do this accurately. Lay out the block pieces on a piece of paper and make sure all the bear claws (half-square triangle units) are oriented correctly.

First, assemble the corner units consisting of the large square, four half-square triangle units, and a small background square. See Figure 1. Join the half-square triangle units together in pairs, and then add the small background corner square to four of them. Sew the pairs without the corner squares onto the big squares and then add the pairs with the corner squares.

Once all these sections are completed, join them in rows with the sashing strips in between and make the center section from two sashing strips and the center square. Then stitch the three rows together to finish the block, and add the borders.

This is an attractive, but relatively complex pattern. Give yourself a pat on the back when it's all done!

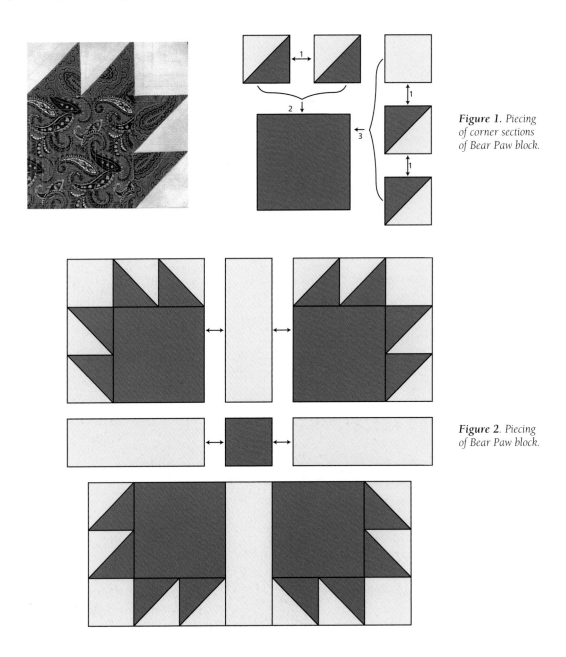

Figure 1. Piecing of corner sections of Bear Paw block.

Figure 2. Piecing of Bear Paw block.

Quarter-Square Triangles

Squares divided in half diagonally both ways into four triangles make quarter-square triangle units. Instructions for piecing these are in Section One, page 28.

Kate, Alicen, Megan, and Megan show their Ohio Star preemie baby blankets.

✂ cutting for Ohio stars

(see page 77 for supplies)

Quarter-square triangle units, star point and background fabrics:
- (2) 7¾" squares of each

Star center:
- (1) 7" square

Background corners:
- (4) 7" squares

Borders:
- (2) 3½" x 20" sides
- (2) 3½" x 26" top and bottom

Ohio Stars

The Ohio Star utilizes quarter-square triangle units to make the star points. The four different Ohio Star quilts shown in this section are all made from the same basic pattern. The appearance of this pattern can change dramatically according to the placement of light and dark fabrics and the variety of fabrics used. In all my examples, the star is made from darker fabric than the background, but you could reverse these and have a dark background with a light star to create a different look. If you would like to experiment with different colors or fabrics, photocopy the Ohio Star in Appendix 9, and color it with crayons or paste your fabrics onto it.

Batik Star preemie baby blanket, 25" x 25".

Sophie's Winter Star doll blanket with hand painted fabric, 25" x 25".

Christmas Star, hand quilted, 25½" x 25½".

The first two quilts use only two fabrics in the star. Sophie printed her own snowflake fabric using the freezer paper reverse stencil technique to make the background for her winter star (see Section One, page 45 for instructions). We decided it wasn't a good idea to give a preemie baby a blanket with paint, so Sophie's lucky doll, Kevin, got it instead!

Make the quarter-square triangle units. These should measure 7" unfinished and fit exactly with the center and corner squares. If they are too small, you may trim the center and corner squares so that they are the same size (remember to adjust the border sizes as necessary). If they are too large, trim them on each side to 7" maintaining the triangle points in the corners. Proceed as for the simple 9-patch and add the borders to complete the quilt top.

This Christmas Star has four different fabrics in the star.

The cutting sizes are the same as those already given, but you will need two squares of star point fabric and one square each of the other two fabrics that appear in the quarter-square triangle unit. Sew one star point fabric square to each of the other squares to make the first sets of paired triangles. Cut and match them up in the correct configuration for your star pattern. The borders on this quilt have cornerstones so cut the four border strips 3½" x 20", and the four cornerstones 3½" square.

The last variation on the Ohio Star theme has fused appliqué hearts in the large squares, and two borders. The binding of pansy fabric gives it an additional narrow frame around the edge. Use the small heart template in Appendix 3. For instructions on fusible appliqué, see Section One, page 43.

Fuse the hearts in the center of each 7" square and stitch around their edges in a machine embroidery stitch or hand sewn blanket stitch. Proceed as for the other Ohio Stars. This makes a particularly decorative little quilt, which you may wish to hang on the wall.

✂ cutting for Valentine's star

(see page 77 for supplies)

Quarter-square triangle units, star point and background fabrics:
- (2) 7¾" squares of each

Center and corner squares:
- (5) 7" squares

Hearts:
- (5) 5" squares backed with Steam-a-Seam 2

Inner border:
- (2) 1½" x 20" sides
- (2) 1½" x 22" top and bottom

Outer border with cornerstones:
- (4) 3¼" x 22" sides
- (4) 3¼" squares, corners

Valentine's Star, commercially quilted, 26¾" x 26¾".

4-Block Quilts and Blankets

A sampler is a quilt in which every block is different. Choose any four of the 9" patchwork blocks shown in Appendix 1, or design your own. The cutting instructions for the blocks are provided in Appendix 2, and Section Two, page 48 gives further details on patchwork blocks. Repeating a couple of blocks, or making the quilt from four blocks of the same pattern, are other options.

The two examples shown here look very different. One is made from calico prints and the blocks are set adjacently. The other is a bit wild looking, made from batik prints, with each block framed and sashing added. The binding in a contrasting color adds another narrow border. Once again, this demonstrates how the choice of fabrics can dramatically affect the whole tone of the quilt.

✂ cutting for 4-block sampler with adjacent blocks

(see page 77 for supplies)

9" blocks:
- (4); cutting instructions in Appendix 2

Inner border:
- (2) 1½" x 18½" sides
- (2) 1½" x 20½" top and bottom

Outer border:
- (2) 3" x 20½" sides
- (2) 3" x 25½" top and bottom

Piece the blocks and then join them in pairs in the desired configuration. Sew the pairs together and add the borders.

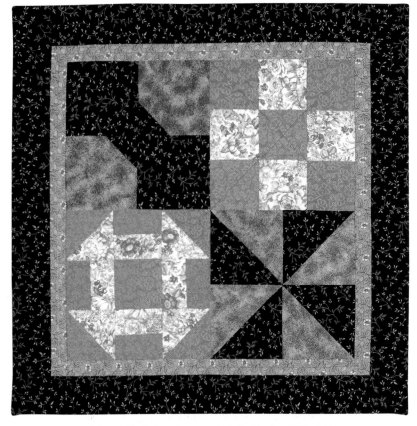

Calico 4-Block Sampler preemie baby blanket, 25" x 25".

instructions

Piece the blocks and add the frames. Join the framed blocks and sashing strips in rows. You should have three rows of sashing (cornerstone, strip, cornerstone, strip, cornerstone), and two rows of blocks (strip, framed block, strip, framed block, strip). Sew the five rows together to complete the assembly of the quilt top.

Donna and Shane show their 4-block preemie baby blankets.

✂ cutting for 4-block sampler with frames and sashing strips

(see page 77 for supplies)

9" blocks:
- (4); cutting instructions in Appendix 2

Block frames:
- (8) 1¼" x 9½" sides (from 2 full-width 1¼" strips)
- (8) 1¼" x 11" tops and bottoms (from 3 full-width 1¼" strips)

Sashing and cornerstones:
- (12) 2½" x 11" strips (from 4 full-width 2½" strips)
- (9) 2½" squares, corners

Batik 4-Block Sampler, machine quilted, 27" x 27".

Crazy Patchwork Quilt

Crazy Patchwork is a great way to use up odd scraps to produce a lively looking quilt. The use of black sashing strips makes the blocks look vibrant. These quilts are fun to embellish with buttons and charms. For instructions on making the 5½" Crazy Patchwork blocks, see Section One, page 29.

instructions

Make nine Crazy Patchwork blocks measuring 6" square (unfinished size). Lay them out in the desired configuration and number them with small sticky labels to help you keep them in the correct order. Sew them in three rows with 6" sashing strips in between (block, sashing, block, sashing, block). Join the rows together with the four 19" sashing strips (sashing, blocks, sashing, blocks, sashing, blocks, sashing). Now add the last two 21" sashing strips to the two sides without sashing. Finish the quilt top by adding the outer border. Buttons and charms will give the little quilt extra pizzazz, and the kids will really enjoy selecting them. Have fun!

cutting

(see page 77 for supplies)

Assorted scraps for blocks:
- 2" x 3" minimum (may be irregularly shaped, with straight edges)

Sashing cut from 4 full-width 1½" strips:
- (6) 1½" x 6"
- (4) 1½" x 19"
- (2) 1½" x 21"

Outer border:
- (2) 2¾" x 21" sides
- (2) 2¾" x 25½" top and bottom

Crazy Patchwork Quilt, envelope style, tied, with buttons and charms added, 25" x 25".

Design Your Own Quilt or Blanket

Laetitia, Megan, Laurel, Layne, Emelie, and Alicen with their own pattern variations.

The possibilities are endless for variations on the preceding patterns and new designs using the basic units of squares, triangles, and rectangles. Here are some wonderful examples made by the creative kids at Hyla Middle School. A couple of these became extremely elaborate and challenging, but the kids had great fun and were very successful. The results are beautiful.

Kate, Alicen, and Megan tuck up the stuffed animals.

Lap Quilts

Ramona and Katie with their lap quilts.

Lap quilts are large enough to snuggle under, but not big enough to cover a bed. Most of the patterns provided are in the 50"- to 55"-square range, but one or two are bigger and almost bed-sized. The piecing techniques are the same as for the little quilts. There are just lots more pieces!

While some of these lap quilts are relatively simple, they are much larger than the other projects in this book. They require more investment in terms of materials and time, so I

recommend that you begin by learning the basic skills on one of the smaller projects. Once you are comfortable using a rotary cutter and you can sew consistently with a ¼" seam allowance, you can make any of these quilts. Setting realistic deadlines often helps you to complete a project, but don't stress out about it—you are supposed to be having fun!

Hyla Middle School students made six of the featured lap quilts. Teacher Chris Johnson organized Quilt Camp for Exploration Week at the end of the school year. The six who signed up (four 6th graders and two 8th graders) went to Fort Worden State Park in Port Townsend, where they stayed for four nights in one of the big, old officers' houses. They spent five days quilting under Chris' guidance and made beautiful lap quilt tops. Most of them were new to quilting, and for all of them, completing a quilt top was a tremendous achievement and a fulfilling experience.

Chris worked with the students before they went to Quilt Camp, helping them choose their patterns. They spent six 40-minute sessions planning their quilts and learning the quilting basics, such as rotary cutting, use of the sewing machines, and practicing strip piecing 4-patches, as well as some color theory. Then the group went on a shopping expedition to buy fabric, and we were surprised by their choices. As you will see, there was a wide range of fabrics selected, some very sophisticated and not what you might expect 11 to 14 year olds to choose. Chris helped them assess the appropriate fabric values for their quilt patterns, and stipulated that the border fabric must be one of the fabrics used in the center field. She also asked that the binding be the same as the outer border. She encouraged them to buy two or three additional fabrics so that there was some scope for trying out different fabric combinations. This was sound advice. It is very difficult to have a complete vision of how all the fabrics will look when they are pieced into blocks to make the patterns. Changing your mind over the details is common during quilting projects, and it is often easier to see ways to improve your plans once you get started. Port Townsend has two fabric stores with a good selection of quilting supplies, so they could go shopping again during Quilt Camp if necessary.

The children began Quilt Camp with their fabrics pre-washed and were eager to start cutting and piecing. They spent several hours each day quilting, but also had time for walks on the beach, flashlight games in the bunkers, and trips into town for ice cream and other goodies. On the way home from Quilt Camp,

Sophie with her lap quilt.

they took their completed quilt tops to Wanda Rains to be commercially machine quilted. The kids were thrilled when their finished quilts were returned. They certainly had good reason to congratulate themselves and to be proud of their accomplishments.

The two 8th graders on the trip, Katie and Ramona, moved on to high school, but returned to Hyla each week in the fall for after-school quilt club. They made baby blankets and helped the younger kids who were just beginning to quilt. We were thrilled by their enthusiasm and desire to participate. Ramona began quilting in 3rd grade, when she was in elementary school at The Family Classroom. I worked there in 1997. The quilts we made, and the children who participated, including Ramona, are featured in my first book, *Creative Quilting with Kids*, (Krause Publications, 2001). It gives me great pleasure to see Ramona continuing to quilt and develop her skills. Ramona and Katie are both accomplished quilters who are well-equipped to embark on projects without any adult help. I applaud their achievements and willingness to mentor beginning students.

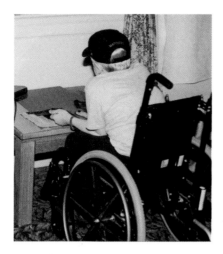

Scenes from Quilt Camp, 2002

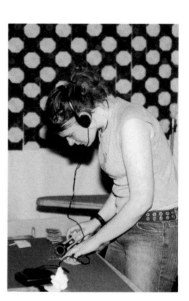

General Instructions and Tips

Don't forget to refer to Section One for all of the detailed instructions on the various piecing and finishing techniques. In all of these quilts, the tops are constructed in rows and follow the method described in detail for the 81-patch. All the quilts are assembled with straight line seams. Wherever possible, press seams so that they butt in opposing directions and lie flat when sewn. Use a quilt wall, or floor space, to arrange the blocks and sashing in the desired orientation, and number the pieces to keep them in order during assembly.

Adding borders onto large quilts can be a little tricky, and accurate measuring is important to prevent the quilt from acquiring wavy edges. The measurements provided in the cutting instructions assume accurate $\frac{1}{4}$" seam allowances for the piecing of the center fields of the quilts. On large quilts, tiny discrepancies on seams add up because there are so many seams. Piece and measure the center field of the quilt before you cut the borders to their exact length. If instructed to cut the border strips before other patchwork pieces of the same fabric, cut the strips the correct width, but wait to cut the precise length until you have pieced and measured the centerfield of the quilt top. Then, it is easy to make adjustments if necessary. Refer to Section One, page 30 for more information on borders. Most borders will be longer than a full width of fabric. Hence, they should either be cut lengthwise from the fabric, or pieced from two strips cut across the width of the fabric. Piecing is fine for many monochromatic or small print fabrics, since it doesn't really show. If you have a distinctive pattern on the fabric, the seam will be more visible. Pieced borders are far more economical on fabric.

The same applies to quilt backs. Nearly all of these quilts are wider than one width of fabric, so two whole quilt lengths of fabric are needed to make the back. However, the back can be pieced from one length plus lengths of the border fabric. As an example, suppose the quilt is 56" x 56" and the outer border is 4" wide. If you buy 1¾ yards each of the backing and border fabric (or 3½ yards of one fabric if the back and border are the same), you will have enough for the backing and the borders. The backing 1¾ yards lies down the middle of the back. The width is 42", so an additional 18" (9" on the two sides) is needed to make the back the desired size (size of quilt top is 56", then adding an extra 2" on each side equals 60"). Cut the selvages off both fabrics. Cut two strips 9½" wide from the full length of the border fabric and join these onto the two sides of the backing piece to complete the back. You still have a piece of border fabric at least 20" x 1¾ yards from which to cut the four 4½" border strips. See Section One, page 31 for more information on quilt backs. A limited choice of 90" and 108" wide cotton is available at most quilt stores and provides an alternative option.

Several of these lap quilts were commercially machine quilted in a variety of all-over patterns. Carol Latham quilted the 81-patch and the Log Cabin variation, and Wanda Rains did all the others. For the quilts that were quilted using a regular sewing machine, quilting details are provided.

The binding fabric does not necessarily have to be the same as the outer border. If you choose a border fabric for your binding, you can cut the binding strips lengthwise after the border strips are cut. Then you should not need to buy any additional binding fabric. For instructions on binding, see Section One, page 40.

Remember to make a label for your quilt—see Section One, page 41. Lap quilts can be hung on the wall if you like—see Section One, page 42 for ways to hang your quilt.

Two of the quilts—the 81-patch and the large Ohio Star—are made from flannel, which kids love. Flannel is wonderfully soft, but a little more difficult to piece accurately. Use it only on quilts with large pieces. Increasing the machine stitch size a tad (to a 3 on a machine with 0-4 as the range) will help. Some flannels are much more stretchy than others, especially when they are sewn on the bias. Flannel may be used for the quilt back with a regular cotton quilt top. I'm just giving you even more options!

81-Patch Quilt

This quilt is made from 81 squares in a 9 x 9 format. It is a fast and simple pattern, and a great way to make a large quilt relatively easily. For instructions on machine piecing the patchwork, refer to Section One, page 23. Like the small 25-patch quilts, there are many ways to create patterns by varying the placement of your colors and light and dark fabrics. You may photocopy and color Appendix 10 to experiment with different color arrangements, for example, diagonal lines of color, checkerboard, 9-patches, or random. Trip Around the World is a traditional quilt pattern in which each layer of color surrounds the center square.

Trip Around the World quilt, made from flannel, commercially quilted, 67½" x 67½".

supplies

Begin by coloring or annotating the 9 x 9 grid (photocopy Appendix 10) and recording how many squares of each color are needed. One full width 8" strip will yield five squares, so you can calculate how much fabric you will need—¼ yard per five squares. I will use my Trip Around the World as an example, beginning with the center color and working out.

- Salmon pink:
  center square + 12 squares in corners = 13 = ¾ yd.
- Green:
  4 around center square + 8 squares in corners = 12 = ¾ yd.
- Gray:
  8 around green + 4 in corners = 12 = ¾ yd.
- Red:
  12 around gray = ¾ yd.
- Blue:
  16 around red = 1 yd. (I actually used 4 different blues and had ¼ yd. of each)
- Purple:
  16 in corners next to blue = 1 yd.
  If I've done my math correctly, that should add up to 81 squares!

You will also need:
- ⅔ yd. binding (¾ yard for flannel)
- 72" x 72" batting
- 4 yd. backing

cutting

Squares:
- (81) 8" squares

instructions

Use a 15" square ruler to cut full-width 8" strips, and then counter-cut the strips to make the squares. Alternatively, use the grid on the cutting mat to measure the 8".

Construction of this quilt is straightforward. When I made my Trip Around the World quilt, I laid all the squares out on the floor and numbered them with small sticky labels, and then stacked them in rows. If you don't do this, it is easy to lose track of the squares and make mistakes with the piecing sequence. Simply join the squares together in rows. Press the seams of rows 1, 3, 5, 7, and 9 in one direction, and the seams of rows 2, 4, 6, and 8 in the opposite direction, so that the seams butt nicely when you assemble the rows. Remove the sticky labels when ironing, so that the heat doesn't leave a gummy residue on the fabric. After pressing each row, replace the first number of the row, so that each row is identifiable. Laying out the completed rows helps too. Double-check the sequence to avoid errors and unsewing. Join the rows in pairs, 1+2, 3+4, 5+6, and 7+8+9, and then join these in pairs being careful to keep them in the right order. The last seam should be across the middle of the quilt between rows 4 and 5. Clear sufficient table space or position a chair nearby to support the weight of the quilt top as it increases in size. This makes accurate sewing much easier.

One Hundred Rectangles

This rectangular quilt is made from 100 rectangles in a 10 x 10 grid. The piecing technique is the same as for the 81-patch above, that is, join the rectangles in rows, press the seams of adjacent rows in opposing directions, and then assemble the rows. There are also two borders to frame the center field. For instructions on machine piecing the patchwork, refer to Section One, page 23.

Sophie made this quilt when she was 10 years old, for a special exhibition "Quilts for the Young at Heart," sponsored by David Textiles, Inc., and displayed at Houston International Quilt Market and Festival in 2001. David Textiles provided all the fabrics to feature their line of Wizard of Oz theme prints. Sophie selected the fabrics for her quilt from their swatch samples. Her color choice is exciting and refreshing. Half of the rectangles are the pictorial Wizard of Oz print with poppies and Oz characters. The other alternating colors read as solids but are all prints, two of them Wizard of Oz and the rest are assorted. Sophie also machine embroidered "Sophie Sleeps in Oz" onto the border of her quilt. The contrast between the pictorial fabric and the alternating colors is what makes this quilt so visually appealing. You could use this idea with any theme print and contrasting fabric, and of course, arrange the colors in any way you choose.

Sophie with her quilt.

Sophie Sleeps in Oz, pieced and machine quilted by Sophie, 61" x 46".

supplies for 100 rectangles (Sophie's format)

- 1 yd. theme fabric for rectangles
- ¼ yd. each, 5 fabrics for the alternate rectangles
- 1¼ yd. inner border (½ yd. if borders are pieced)
- 1⅓ yd. outer border
- ½ yd. binding
- 65" x 50" batting
- 3¾ yd. backing

cutting for 100 rectangles (Sophie's format)

Theme fabric:
    (50) 5½" x 4" rectangles (from 5 full-width 5½" strips)

Alternating fabrics:
    (10) 5½" x 4" rectangles of each of the 5 fabrics (from 1 full-width 5½" strip of each)

Inner border:
    (2) 2" x 50½" sides
    (2) 2" x 38½" top and bottom

Outer border:
    (2) 4½" x 53½" sides
    (2) 4½" x 46½" top and bottom

ABOVE: *Detail of embroidered lettering.*

BELOW: *Detail of binding.*

instructions

Piece the quilt in rows (just like the 81-patch, see page 106), and then add the borders. Sophie machine embroidered her lettering on the border strip before joining the strip to the quilt. For instructions on machine embroidery, see Section One, page 20. Sophie machine quilted a serpentine stitch along the seam lines. She sewed the binding to the back, and then brought it to the front and top-stitched it with a zigzag stitch.

4-Patch

The 4-patch is a great beginning project with scope for playing around with the pattern by rotating the 4-patches. The blocks are easy to construct using strip piecing (see page 25 for instructions), and simple to join alternately with the large squares. This is one of the few lap quilts in the book with a backing less than 42" wide, so the back does not need to be pieced.

The quilt featured is made in a 5 x 7 grid with a total of (18) 4-patches and 17 large squares. The blocks are 6½" square. To make a quilt of a similar size in a 7 x 9 grid, the block size would be 5" square (cut 4-patch strips 3" wide and big squares 5½"). Photocopy and color the grid in Appendix 11 to try out your color schemes. The grid can be cut down to the desired size and blocks cut out. Turning the 4-patches will generate new patterns. In the example shown, I have alternated the direction of the pale squares in the 4-patches along diagonal lines. Notice how in the 4-patches with the yellow triangle fabric, the other squares are so similar to the large squares, that they merge into the background, and the yellow squares really pop out.

This quilt (technically, a comforter) is tied with variegated pearl cotton (see page 39 for tying instructions). I used extra loft (Mountain Mist Fat Batt) polyester batting to make it poofy. The flannel backing makes it especially cozy.

4-patch and Squares comforter, tied, 53" x 40".

instructions

Strip piece the 4-patches and then lay the pieces out in the desired configuration. Number the 4-patches and squares with small sticky labels and proceed as for the 81-patch, page 106. When pressing the rows, iron the seams away from the 4-patches and toward the large squares. Add the borders to complete the quilt top.

supplies for 4-patch and squares

- ¼ yd. pieces for 4-patches in a variety of fabrics (6 used in the example shown. ¼ yd. is enough for 10 blocks. If only 2 fabrics are used, you'll need ½ yd. of each).
- 1½ yd. borders and large squares
- ½ yd. binding
- 54" x 44" batting (extra loft fat batt polyester for poofy look)
- 1 skein of 5g multicolored pearl cotton for tying
- 1¾ yd. backing (flannel optional)

cutting for 4-patch and squares

Calculate the number of 4-patches of each color combination. Each pair of strips yields (5) 4-patches and a total of (18) 4-patches are needed.

4-patches with 2 fabrics only:
- 4 full width 3¾" strips of each

Borders and large squares (cut the border strips lengthwise before cutting the large squares):
- (2) 4" x 46" sides
- (2) 4" x 40" top and bottom
- (17) 7" squares

Rail Fence

The Rail Fence is a strip pieced project made from four strips. It is fast and relatively easy to complete. There are 30 blocks set in a 5 x 6 grid. By alternating the orientation of the blocks, a secondary zigzag pattern emerges across the quilt top. Placement of colors in the strip sequence is important. The two fabrics on the outer edges of the sequence form the zigzags. The middle two do not connect with adjacent blocks so are sandwiched between the zigzags. Grading the sequence from dark to light works well, as well as using what we call "zinger" fabrics—ones that act as an accent or contrast in the zigzags. See Section One, page 25 for instructions on strip piecing.

supplies

- ¾ yd. each of 4 fabrics, strips
- 1½ yd. each of 2 border fabrics (if these are the same as 2 of the strips fabrics, 1½ yd. is sufficient for the borders and strips; cut the borders lengthwise before cutting the strips).
- ⅔ yd. binding, if different from backing
- 62" x 54" batting
- 3½ yd. backing (includes enough for binding)

 ## cutting

Strips, four fabrics:
- 8 full-width 2½" strips of each

Inner border:
- (2) 2½" x 40½" top and bottom
- (2) 2½" x 48½" sides

Outer border:
- (2) 3½" x 40½" top and bottom
- (2) 3½" x 48½" sides

Corners:
- (4) 5½" squares

instructions

Sew the eight sets of four strips in the desired sequence. Press all the seams in the same direction from the back and then thoroughly press from the front, making sure the strips are parallel and straight. The strip sets should be 8½" wide if the piecing is accurate. Counter-cut them 8½" to make 30 square blocks. If your strip widths are, for example, consistently 8¼" instead of 8½", counter-cut 8¼" to make the blocks square. Blocks measuring 8½" x 8¼" don't go together very easily! The 15" square is the best ruler to use for cutting. Lay the blocks in the correct configuration. Each alternate block is turned 90 degrees. Proceed as for the 81-patch, page 106. When pressing the rows, iron the seams away from the blocks with horizontal strips and toward the blocks with vertical strips.

Sew the inner and outer border strips together before joining them to the center field. Adjust their length, if necessary. The corner squares should be added to the top and bottom borders. Join the side borders to the quilt top first, and then add the top and bottom borders with the corner squares. I quilted this quilt with a straight stitch in the center of the zigzags and in the ditch between the middle strips in each block.

Rail Fence, machine quilted, 58" x 50".

Snowball

This Snowball pattern is the same as the pattern for the penguin little quilt, (see page 90). The squares are even the same size—there are just lots more of them! There are 25 pictures of animals, alternated with pale units, making a total of 49 Snowballs in a 7 x 7 grid. The small triangles are pieced using the corner triangle method. See Section One, page 27 for instructions.

I made this quilt as a gift for my goddaughter, Tamsin, who loves animals. It was fun going through my stash of fabrics and searching for a variety. Originally, I was going to have animals in every Snowball unit, alternating darks and lights, but the whole thing started to become too busy with too many animals. I opted for animals on relatively dark backgrounds alternating with a light fabric. The orange and blue corner triangles add interest and brighten the pattern. You could use one theme fabric, or maybe three to five fabrics for the pictorial units, instead of lots of different ones. Feel free to adapt the pattern to your liking.

supplies

- 1¼ yd. theme fabric, or a selection of assorted fabrics
- 1¼ yd. light or contrasting fabric to go between pictorials, or a selection of assorted fabrics
- ⅔ yd. each of 2 fabrics for the corner triangles
- 1½ yd. narrow border (enough for 1 set of corner triangles too). Cut border strips lengthwise first
- 1¾ yd. wide border (enough for the binding too)
- ⅔ yd. binding in a different fabric
- 64" x 64" batting
- 3¾ yd. backing

cutting

Pictorial squares:
- (25) 7½" squares

Light squares:
- (24) 7½" squares (from 5 full-width 7½" strips)

Corner triangles, cut from 7 full-width 2¾" strips of each fabric
- (100) 2¾" squares, corners of pictorial squares
- (96) 2¾" squares, corners of light squares

Inner border:
- (2) 1¾" x 49½" sides
- (2) 1¾" x 52" top and bottom

Outer border:
- (2) 4¼" x 52" sides
- (2) 4¼" x 59½" top and bottom

instructions

Begin by attaching all the corner triangles to make the Snowballs. Press the seams toward the pictorial prints and away from the pale alternating prints. Then proceed as for the 81-patch quilt (see page 106). Complete the quilt top by adding the borders. Don't forget to measure the center field and adjust the border lengths if necessary (see Section One, page 30 for further details). I quilted Tamsin's quilt with a serpentine stitch in variegated rayon thread.

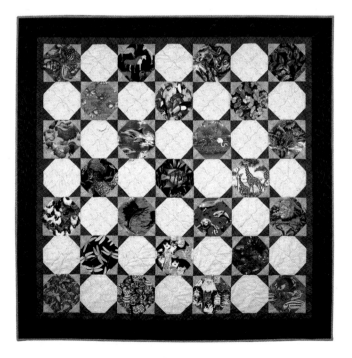

Tamsin's quilt; machine quilted with a serpentine stitch in variegated thread, 59" x 59".

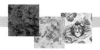

Large Ohio Star

In this quilt, the Ohio Star block has been enlarged to 27", and wide borders added. This lap quilt has relatively few pieces and is another fast one to piece. The star points are made from quarter-square triangles.

See Section One, page 28 for instructions on making these. The design is striking especially if highly contrasting colors or values are used for the star and the background. This is a good candidate for flannel.

supplies
- ¾ yd. star and border corners
- ⅔ yd. background to star
- 1 yd. inner border and binding
- 1 yd. outer side panels
- 55" x 55" batting
- 3¼ yd. backing

 ### cutting
(see page 77 for supplies)

Star fabric:
- (1) 9½" center square
- (2) 10¼" squares for star points

Background:
- (4) 9½" squares, corners of blocks
- (2) 10¼" squares for star points

Inner border:
- (4) 3½" x 27½" strips
- (4) 3½" squares, corners

Outer side panels:
- (4) 9½" x 33½" (cut lengthwise down 1 yd. of fabric)

Outer corner squares:
- (4) 9½" squares

instructions

The 15" square is the best ruler to use when rotary cutting all these large squares. First, make the quarter-square triangle units for the star points. Join these in rows with the 9½" squares and press the seams away from the quarter-square triangle units and toward the big squares. Assemble the rows and then add the borders. For each border, sew the corner squares onto both ends of the top and bottom strips and join these after you have sewn the side strips onto the quilt top.

I also pieced the back of this quilt for economical use of fabric. I had two and one half yards of the outer panel fabric and one yard each of the other three fabrics. This was enough for the entire quilt including the backing and binding. For a picture of this quilt back and more information, see Section One, page 31. I quilted this star with serpentine stitches along the seam lines and radiating out from the center.

Bright Star, flannel, machine quilted with serpentine stitch, 51" x 51".

Two More Star Quilts

Layne and Laurel made these beautiful Star quilts at Quilt Camp under Chris Johnson's supervision. They each selected their own fabrics and, as you can see, they enjoy very different palettes.

In both quilts, the star points are made from corner-square triangles. For instructions, see Section One, page 27. In Layne's quilt, the smaller of the two, the star points are relatively small and do not reach the edges of the blocks, so that the stars appear to float on the background. Laurel's quilt has larger stars with points extending all the way to the edges of the blocks. The Star blocks in both quilts are alternated with 9-patch blocks consisting of small 4-patches in the corners and five squares. Strip piecing is used to make the small 4-patches, see Section One, page 25 for instructions. The squares in the 9-patch blocks form diagonal lines across the quilt top and unify the design, making a delightful setting to display the stars.

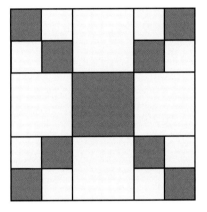

9-patch.

Laurel's Star.

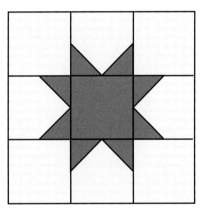

Layne's Star.

Layne's Stars

Layne's quilt consists of nine 9" blocks (five star blocks, and four 9-patch blocks), with a border and corner squares. The blocks blend very nicely since she has used the same background fabric throughout, and their boundaries are not immediately obvious. The stars and squares stand out because of their contrast with the background fabric. This is the smallest of the lap quilt patterns. Layne displays hers as a wall hanging and it is most attractive.

Layne and Laurel with their star quilts.

supplies for Layne's stars

- 1¼ yd. background fabric for stars, 9-patches, and inner border
- ⅓ yd. 9-patch dark squares
- ¼ yd. assorted fabrics for stars (to make all the stars from one fabric, ¼ yd. is sufficient).
- 1 yd. outer border strips and binding
- ¼ yd. corner squares
- 42" x 42" batting
- 1¼ yd. backing

cutting for Layne's star

Background fabric:
- (56) 3½" squares cut from 6 full-width 3½" strips (40 for the 5 star blocks and 16 for (4) 9-patches)
- 2 full-width 2" strips for the small 4-patches
- (2) 2" x 27½" narrow inner borders, sides
- (2) 2" x 30½" top and bottom

9-patch dark squares:
- 2 full-width 2" strips for small 4-patches
- (4) 3½" squares for the centers

Stars:
- (5) 3½" squares for the centers
- (40) 2" squares for the star points cut from 2 full-width 2" strips (for 5 different fabrics, cut 8 squares of each)

Outer border strips:
- (4) 5" x 30½"

Corner squares:
- (4) 5" square

Layne's Stars, commercially quilted, 39" x 39".

instructions

Begin by constructing the smallest components— the 4-patches and the star points. Sew the two sets of 2" strips for the 4-patches and press the seams towards the dark fabric. Counter-cut the strip sets 2" to make 32 rectangles composed of two squares. Join these in pairs to make (16) 4-patches. Make the corner triangle star points using four background 3½" squares and eight star point 2" squares for each block.

Lay out the blocks in their correct configuration and assemble them as you would a simple 9-patch (there should be nine pieces to assemble for each block). The five star blocks and four 9-patch blocks should all measure 9½" (unfinished size). Now, join the blocks into rows and then join the rows. Add the inner border, sides first and then the top and bottom. Complete the quilt by joining the outer border strips and corner squares (sides first, and then the top and bottom with the corner squares attached). Since the quilt is smaller than 42", it is not necessary to piece any of the borders or the back.

Laurel's Stars

Laurel made her vibrant quilt from (25) 9" blocks, 13 stars, and (12) 9-patches. Her star blocks look much larger than Layne's, but this is an illusion because the center of the star is larger and the star points extend all the way to the edges of the block. The stars are bigger, but the blocks are the same size.

Laurel's Stars, commercially quilted, 60" x 60".

supplies for Laurel's stars

- 2 yd. background fabric for stars, 9-patches, and inner border
- ½ yd. 9-patch dark squares
- 1¼ yd. assorted fabrics for stars (¼ yd. yields 3 stars) There are 13 stars. Laurel made 4 orange, 4 pink, 2 yellow, 2 blue, and 1 purple. Calculate your needs according to the number of stars of each fabric.
- 1½ yd. middle border (enough for stars too). Cut border strips lengthwise first.
- 1¾ yd. outer border and binding (enough for 9-patch dark squares or stars too). Cut border strips and binding lengthwise first.
- 64" x 64" batting
- 3¾ yd. backing

instructions

For fabrics used in both the blocks and the border strips, cut the border strips lengthwise first so that they do not have to be pieced. The strips you need for the blocks may also be cut lengthwise since, having cut the borders, your fabric will no longer be 42" wide. The message here is to think ahead, and plan before you cut!

For the background fabric, cut 50" from the two-yard piece. Cut four border strips lengthwise (2" x 50") and set them aside until the center of the quilt top is complete (see General Instructions and Tips, page 105). You are left with two pieces of fabric measuring approximately 50" x 33" and 22" x 42". Use the 50" piece to cut the remaining background pieces lengthwise, except for the rectangles, which should be cut from full-width strips (the 22" x 42" piece).

Follow the same piecing instructions as for Layne's Star, page 114. Instead of 3 x 3 blocks, there are 5 x 5 blocks. One of Laurel's blue fabrics had silver and colored stars stuck onto the surface. While these looked awesome, they melted when they were ironed on the right side, and caused some problems. Let this be a warning to you when you are selecting your fabrics!

cutting for Laurel's stars

Background fabric:
- Inner borders cut lengthwise from 50" piece:
    - (2) 2" x 45½" sides
    - (2) 2" x 48½" top and bottom
- 9-patches (12 blocks):
    - 4 lengthwise 50" x 2" strips for 4-patches
    - (48) 3½" squares for corners cut from 4 lengthwise 50" x 3½" strips
- Stars (13 blocks):
    - (52) 2¾" squares cut from 3 lengthwise 50" x 2¾" strips
    - (52) 5" x 2¾" rectangles cut from 4 full-width 5" strips (use the 22" x 42" piece)

9-patch dark squares:
- (12) 3½" squares for centers, cut from 1 full-width 3½" strip
- 5 full-width 2" strips for 4-patches. Piece with background 4-patch strips and counter-cut (96) 2" to make (48) 4-patches

Stars:
- (1) 5" square and (8) 2¾" squares for each block. Cut strips and counter cut the squares for multiple blocks of one fabric. Total of (13) 5" center squares and (104) 2¾" squares for star points.

Middle border:
- (2) 2" x 48½" sides
- (2) 2" x 51½" top and bottom

Outer border:
- (2) 5" x 51½" sides
- (2) 5" x 60½" top and bottom

Katie's True Lover's Knot

The True Lover's Knot is a variation of the Bowtie pattern. The background to the Bowtie is made up of 4-patches instead of single squares. The corner square triangles are attached to the 4-patches to complete the Bowties (see page 27), and strip piecing is used to make the 4-patches (see page 25). The orientation of the Bowties creates a secondary larger pattern, the True Lover's Knot. This big quilt could be used on a bed. It is probably the longest project in this book and the one with the most repetitious piecing. There are 360 corner square-triangles and (77) 4-patches! Though not difficult, it requires patience and persistence, but the end product is a beautiful quilt. You need good organizational skills to cut and keep track of all the pieces. Katie was renowned for her assembly line piecing at Quilt Camp, and she enjoyed making really long chains of 4-patches!

The pattern is composed of 154 units, 77 squares of theme fabric, alternating with (77) 4-patches with corner square triangles in an 11 x 14 grid, plus 50 half-units round the edges. Katie chose a dark blue celestial theme fabric, which she also used for the outer border, backing, and binding. Her 4-patches are made from two pale fabrics, a green, and a yellow. The contrast between the pale background and the dominant blue star fabric makes the pattern jump out, and it is striking.

Katie's True Lover's Knot,
commercially quilted, 74" x 62".

Katie and Chris.

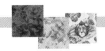

supplies

- 7¼ yd. theme fabric (2½ yards for squares, side rectangles, and corner square triangles, 4¾ yd. for backing, outer border, and binding)*
- 1 yd. of each, 2 light fabrics for 4-patches
- 1¾ yd. inner border (or ½ yd. if border strips are pieced)
- 2 yd. middle border (or 1 yd. if border strips are pieced)
- 78" x 66" batting

*My advice is to ask the fabric store to cut the 7¼-yard hunk of fabric into more conveniently sized pieces—one 2½ yards, two 2¼ yards, and one ¼ yard, or you can do this yourself. Then it is much easier to iron and cut. Use the 2½-yard piece to cut the 4½" squares, side rectangles, and squares for the corner triangles. The other bits are for the backing, outer border strips, and binding.

instructions

Begin by strip piecing the 4-patches. Join the 12 sets of pale strips, press the seams toward the darker fabric, and counter-cut them 2½". A total of 179 of these rectangles are needed—154 to make the (77) 4-patches and 25 for the ½-units around the sides of the center field. Add the theme fabric corner triangles to all the corners of the (77) 4-patches, two corners on each side unit, and one corner on each of the two pale corner squares.

Lay out the 4-patches, theme squares, side rectangles, and corner squares in the correct configuration. You may use the photograph of the quilt as a guide, or design your own pattern. Number all the units with small sticky labels and piece them in rows just like the 81-patch, page 106, and then assemble the rows. Once the center field of the quilt top is completed, add the borders, sides first and then the tops and bottoms. Check your measurements, and adjust the border sizes if necessary (see Section One, page 30). You deserve many congratulations when you have completed this quilt!

✂ cutting

Theme fabric:
- (77) 4½" squares cut from 10 full width 4-1/2" strips
- (25) 2½" x 4½" rectangles cut from 2 full-width 4½" strips
- (2) 2" squares, corners
- (360) 1½" squares for corner triangles, cut from 14 full-width 1½" strips

Light fabrics, 4-patches and side rectangles:
- 12 full-width 2½" strips of each
- (1) 2½" square of each, corners

Inner border:
- (2) 1½" x 60½" sides
- (2) 1½" x 50½" top and bottom

Middle border:
- (2) 5" x 62½" sides
- (2) 5" x 59½" top and bottom

Outer border (cut lengthwise from one of 2¼ yard pieces):
- (2) 2" x 71½" sides
- (2) 2" x 62½" top and bottom

Backing: Use the same piece of fabric that you used to cut the outer borders and cut it lengthwise, 25" wide. Join onto the other 2¼ yd. full width piece to make the backing.

Binding: Cut the binding from the remains of the 2¼ piece and use the ¼ yd. piece of fabric for additional binding strips (you will need at least 1 and probably 2 or 3 binding strips from the ¼ yd.).

Katie with her long chain of piecing.

Ramona's Milky Way

The Milky Way pattern looks very complicated because the edges of the blocks appear to merge. The (16) 9" blocks are 9-patches composed of a center square, four ½-Square triangle units (see Section One, page 27), and four 4-patches (see Section One, page 25). The sashing strips, made from 3" squares and 3" half-square triangle units, create stars between the blocks. This generates a tessellated pattern and it looks as though the blocks overlap. Ramona's use of contrasting values in her fabric selection is excellent and, as a result, the pattern looks rich. She made this quilt at Quilt Camp.

The diagram on page 121 illustrates four 9-patches and the way in which the sashing strips form a star between these blocks. Ramona's quilt has (16) 9-patch blocks (4 x 4), separated by pieced sashing strips, making a total of 25 stars.

Ramona's Milky Way, commercially quilted, 59" x 59".

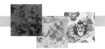

supplies

- 2 yd. pale background fabric
- 1 yd. dark 4-patch squares
- 1¼ yd. assorted dark fabrics for stars (¼ yd. is enough to make 6 stars)
- 1½ yd. narrow border (or ½ yd. if border is pieced)
- 1¾ yd. outer border and binding
- 64" x 64" batting
- 3¾ yd. backing

Note: The squares to make the half-square triangle units should be cut 3⅞". If your seam allowances are exactly ¼", these units will measure 3½" unfinished. If you are concerned that your seam allowances may be inconsistent, cut the squares larger, 4" or even 4¼", and then trim each completed half-square triangle unit to exactly 3½", maintaining the triangle points in the corners. Try this out for one or two to see what works best for you before you cut all the squares. It is better to have a unit that needs to be trimmed, than one that is too small. Trimming them all seems tedious, but they will be really accurate and easy to assemble with the 4-patches and squares.

✂ cutting

Background fabric:
- 13 full width 2" strips for 4-patches
- (56) 3⅞" squares for half-square triangle units cut from 6 full-width 3⅞" strips
- (24) 3½" squares for sashing cut from 3 full-width 3½" strips

Dark squares in 4-patches:
- 13 full-width 2" strips

25 Stars:
- (1) 3½" center square and (2) 3⅞" squares for star points for each star. Total of (25) 3½" squares and (50) 3⅞". Cut an additional (6) 3⅞" squares for the 12 star point units around the edge. Use assorted dark fabrics to make a variety of stars.

Inner border (Cut lengthwise from fabric, or crosswise and join):
- (2) 2" x 45½" sides
- (2) 2" x 48½" top and bottom.

Outer border (Cut lengthwise and use the left over piece to cut the binding):
- (2) 6" x 48½" sides
- (2) 6" x 59½" top and bottom.

instructions

Begin by piecing all of the 4-patches. Join the 13 pairs of dark and background strips. Press the seams toward the dark fabric and counter-cut 2" to make 128 rectangles. Assemble the (64) 4-patches. They should measure 3½" unfinished. Next, piece the half-square triangle units. These should also measure 3½" unfinished (see above). There are 25 stars and each one has four half-square triangle units. For each star, use two star point squares and two background squares to make the four units. In addition to these 100 half-square triangle units, you need 12 more for the partial stars (points only) around the edge (in the sashing). Assemble the (16) 9-patches and then lay out all the blocks and sashing strip pieces in the correct configuration. Another star is made at

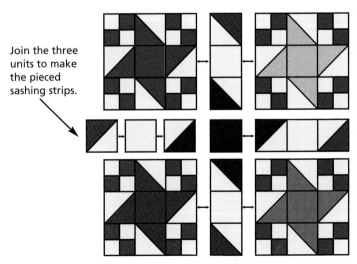

Join the three units to make the pieced sashing strips.

Join the blocks and pieced sashing in rows.

each sashing intersection (nine of these). Use the quilt photograph, and the diagram of the blocks and sashing layout to help you.

Join the sashing pieces into three-piece sections, (half-square triangle unit, background square, half-square triangle unit), being careful to maintain the correct orientation of the triangles. You should have 24 of these sections to go in between the blocks, 12 between the sides of the blocks, and 12 between the rows of the blocks. Place the completed sections back into your layout. Put numbered sticky labels on the blocks, pieced sashing strips, and sashing intersections (squares of star fabric) to help you keep them in the right order. Join them all in rows. There are four rows of blocks and pieced sashing, alternating with three rows of pieced sashing with intersecting squares. Be careful to join the rows in the correct order so that the star points in the sashing match their center squares at the sashing intersections. This all sounds rather complicated, but if you lay all the pieces out and work methodically, using the pictures and diagram as a pattern guide, it should all make sense! The worst that can happen, as Ramona discovered, is the need for some frog stitching—rip-it, rip-it, rip-it!

Add the borders to your center field to complete the quilt top. The piecing of this quilt is not difficult, but keeping the pieces in the right order is the challenge. It is definitely worth the time and effort to stay well organized to construct this stunning pattern.

Ramona and Katie.

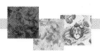

Connor's Log Cabin, commercially quilted, 51½" x 51½".

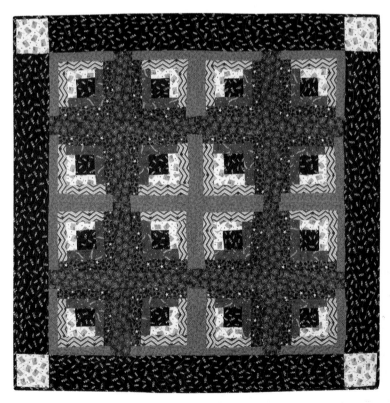

Susie's Log Cabin, commercially quilted, 49" x 49".

Log Cabin Quilts

Connor and Susie made these gorgeous Log Cabin quilts at Quilt Camp. They are a wonderful illustration of two Log Cabin settings creating very different patterns. Look at the choices these two 6th graders made for their fabrics: Connor's reflects a mature, sophisticated palette that blends and pleases. Susie went patriotic, and her inclusion of the pale, zigzag fabric brings delightful energy and life to her quilt. Both are extremely successful.

There are numerous ways to arrange 16 Log Cabin blocks, and you can have fun playing with them. The blocks consist of a center square surrounded by dark logs on two adjacent sides and light logs on the other two sides. The light logs are graded from very light in the center, to medium light on the outer edge. The darks are graded from medium dark in the center to very dark on the edge. The logs are sewn in sequence in layers onto the center square.

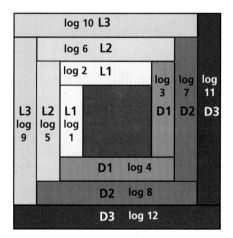

The arrangement of the lights and darks in the log cabin is similar to half-square triangle units made from light and dark triangles. Use the grid of 16 half-square triangles found in Appendix 8 to try different arrangements of multiple blocks on paper and

supplies

- ¼ yd. center squares of Log Cabin blocks
- ½ yd. of each log fabric: 3 dark fabrics (graded medium dark to very dark) and 3 light fabrics (graded very light to medium light)
- 1¼ yd. inner border for Connor's quilt (or ½ yd. if border is pieced)
- 1¼ yd. outer border and binding
- ¼ yd. cornerstones (or use L1 or L2 – there will be enough)
- 55" x 55" batting
- 3 yd. backing

get an approximation of the pattern. Photocopy, color it, and cut the units apart so that you can rearrange them into your own designs. You don't have to make a decision on the quilt layout before you sew the blocks. Simply have fun trying out different possibilities with the blocks, and choose the pattern you like the best.

instructions

Add the Logs in numerical order, beginning with #1 and ending with #12, onto the center square. You can assembly line piece all 16 of them each time.

If you cut the logs to the right size before you started sewing, they should fit exactly. After attaching all the Logs 1 onto their center squares, press the seams toward the logs and add Logs 2 to an adjacent side. Continue in this fashion, always pressing the seams toward the logs and then adding the next batch onto the adjacent side. Once you have completed one row (Logs 1-4) around the middle square, add Logs 5 onto the Logs 1, and so you keep going around until all 12 logs are joined to complete the blocks. Use the block diagram above to help you if you are unsure about the order of the logs.

If you have cut the strips and not the logs, sew the center squares onto L1 strips leaving a gap of ¼" to ½" between each one. Press the seam allowance toward L1. Use a ruler and rotary cut-

cutting

Center Squares of Log Cabin blocks:
- (16) 3" squares

Logs, full-width 1¾" strips:
- L1–4, L2–6, L3–8, D1–5, D2–6, D3–8
  Trim the logs to size after the strips are attached to the block. Alternatively, cut the logs to the exact sizes (only if your seam allowance is an accurate ¼"). Cut the same number of strips as above, then counter-cut (see numbering of the logs in the diagram).

Logs, cut from 1¾" strips:
- L1, Log 1 (16) 1¾" x 3"
- L1, Log 2 (16) 1¾" x 4¼"
- D1, Log 3 (16) 1¾" x 4¼"
- D1, Log 4 (16) 1¾" x 5½"
- L2, Log 5 (16) 1¾" x 5½"
- L2, Log 6 (16) 1¾" x 6¾"
- D2, Log 7 (16) 1¾" x 6¾"
- D2, Log 8 (16) 1¾" x 8"
- L3, Log 9 (16) 1¾" x 8"
- L3, Log 10 (16) 1¾" x 9¼"
- D3, Log 11 (16) 1¾" x 9¼"
- D3, Log 12 (16) 1¾" x 10½"

Inner border (Connor's quilt):
- (2) 1¾" x 40½" sides
- (2) 1¾" x 43" top and bottom

Connor's outer border:
- (4) 5" x 43" cut lengthwise and use the leftover piece for binding

Susie's outer border:
- (4) 5" x 40½"

Corner squares on outer border (both quilts):
- (4) 5" squares

ter to accurately separate and trim the ends of the logs on the 16 block starts so that they are the same length as the center square. Make sure you keep them square by lining up a horizontal line on the ruler with a seam line as well as the edge of the ruler where you are cutting. Next, use L1 strips again to make Log 2 on each block. Sew the center squares with Logs 1 onto the L1 strip, just as you did before, making sure that Log 2 is on an adjacent side to Log 1. Press and trim in the same way. Continue adding strips, pressing the seams toward the strips, and trimming. D1 strips make logs 3 and 4, L2 strips make Logs 5 and 6, D2 strips make Logs

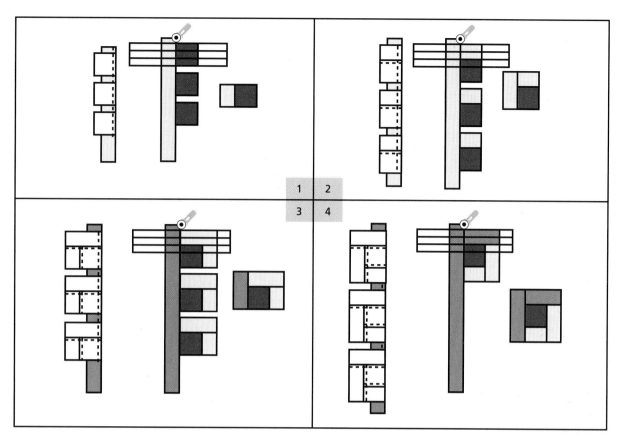

Construction of log cabin blocks using strips.

7 and 8, L3 strips make Logs 9 and 10, and D3 strips make Logs 11 and 12. If this description is hard for you to visualize, I hope the diagram above will help.

Completing 16 Log Cabin blocks is quite an achievement. Enjoy playing with the block orientations until you find your favorite pattern. Number the blocks with sticky labels and proceed as for the 81-patch. Add the borders to complete the quilt top.

Susie and Connor with their quilts.

Log Cabin blocks can be modified relatively easily to produce different patterns. Happy Birthday Infinity is an example of how these traditional blocks can be transformed into something with a much more contemporary look.

I made this quilt for David Textiles, Inc., using their new fabric line "Infinity." Not only did I design the quilt, but the fabric too! The pattern looks complex, but is actually a fairly simple variation of the Log Cabin. It is composed of (16) 12" Log Cabin blocks, eight in which the center square has two frames or layers of logs, and eight in which there are three frames or layers of logs. The strips or logs vary in width and the placement of the striped fabrics adds visual texture and excitement. Instead of using light and dark logs on the sides of the center square, each layer of logs is made from the same fabric so that they look like stacked boxes, or concentric squares. The back of the quilt is pieced from 16 large squares, see page 32 for a photo and further details.

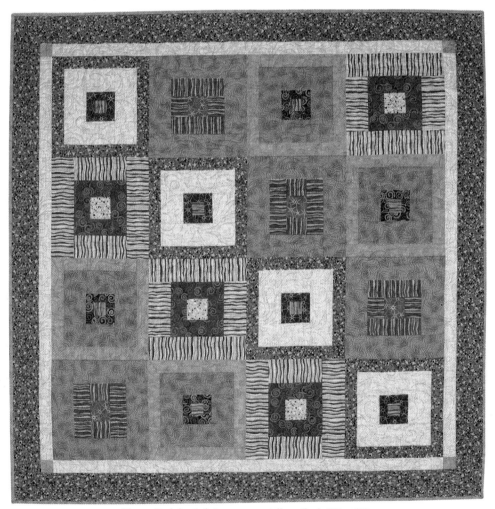

Happy Birthday Infinity, commercially quilted, 58" x 58".

Design Your Own Quilt or Blanket

You can take any of the ideas in this book and use them to create your own quilt designs. The little quilt patterns may be extended and enlarged, or you can combine the things you like from several quilts. Pick two quilt blocks, for example, the 9-patch and the star, and alternate them to see what kinds of patterns emerge. Make a sampler quilt from the different block patterns provided. Turn your blocks on point, add frames around them, or make pieced sashing to create new patterns such as the stars between the blocks on the Milky Way quilt. Don't be afraid to experiment. There are so many possibilities. Have fun!

Alicen designs her own lap quilt. Project in process, Quilt Camp 2003.

Glossary

4-patch block: Block divided into four equal parts (2 x 2).

9-patch block: Block divided into nine equal parts (3 x 3).

16-patch block: Block divided into 16 equal parts (4 x 4).

Adults: Grown-ups who are children at heart!

Appliqué: Process of sewing small pieces of fabric onto a larger background piece of fabric.

Assembly line piecing: Machine piecing several units of fabric together one after another without lifting the presser foot or cutting the threads between units.

Basting: Process of joining the layers of a quilt together to secure them for quilting. Long running stitches sewn by hand, safety pins, or plastic tacks may be used.

Batt: A piece of batting for a quilt.

Batting: (also known as wadding): Fiber used as filling between the quilt top and the quilt backing to provide warmth. It may be cotton, polyester, cotton-polyester blend, wool, or silk.

Betweens: Short, firm needles for hand quilting. The higher the number, the smaller the needle.

Bias: Diagonal grain in relation to the lengthwise and crosswise grains of a woven fabric.

Binding: Narrow strip of fabric used to cover the raw edges and batting of a quilt. Also, the technique of finishing the edges of the quilt.

Block: Design unit of a quilt top. It may be made of patchwork, appliqué, or a combination, and is often square.

Border: Strip of fabric, which may be pieced, framing the outer edges of a quilt top.

Crazy patchwork: Patchwork made from irregular-shaped pieces.

Cross grain: Woven threads of a fabric that are perpendicular to the selvages.

Cutting mat: Special mat used for rotary cutting to protect the surface beneath the fabric and preserve the sharpness of the blade on the cutter.

Embroidery: Process of sewing decorative stitches.

Envelope style: The way in which quilts, blankets, or pillow cover tops may be sewn to their backs, right sides together, and then turned right sides out.

Fat quarter: 18" x 22" piece of fabric (quarter of a yard).

Finished size: Measurements of a completed piece, block, or quilt top without the seam allowances.

Freezer paper: Butcher paper waxed on one side. Used for stabilizing the fabric during drawing or writing, and in the resist stencil printing technique.

Fusible appliqué: Appliqué using fusible webbing to bond the pieces to the background.

Half-square triangle: Triangle made by cutting a square diagonally in half.

Lengthwise grain: Woven fabric threads that run parallel to the selvages.

On point: Block setting in which the block is placed with its sides at 45 degrees to the edge of the quilt.

Patch: Individual fabric shape to be used in patchwork.

Patchwork: Fabric made up of small pieces of fabric sewn together.

Piecing: Joining of patchwork pieces by hand or machine stitching.

Quarter-square triangle: Triangle made by cutting a square diagonally into quarters.

Quilt: Two layers of fabric (the top and the backing), separated by a layer of batting and joined together with quilting stitches.

Quilting: Act of securing the three layers of the quilt together with quilting stitches. Also, the act of making a quilt.

Quilting frame: Large, freestanding frame used for holding the layers of the quilt together for quilting.

Quilting hoop: Tool used to hold a small portion of the quilt taut for quilting.

Quilting stitches: Small stitches that hold the three layers of the quilt together and may also form decorative patterns.

Quilting thread: Special type of thread used for hand quilting, usually stronger than regular sewing thread.

Quilt top: Completed patchwork, appliqué, or whole-cloth top of the quilt that is ready to be joined to the batting and backing to make the quilt.

Quilt wall: An area of wall covered with batting or flannel onto which patchwork pieces and blocks will adhere.

Right side: Front or top of the fabric.

Rotary cutter: Fabric cutting tool with a circular blade that may be used to cut through several layers of fabric at once.

Sampler quilt: Quilt in which all the blocks are of differing patterns.

Sashing: Strip of fabric pieced between two blocks to separate them.

Seam allowance: Margin of fabric between the seam and the raw edge (standard is ¼").

Selvage: Lengthwise finished edge on each side of the fabric.

Snippets: Small pieces of fabric backed with fusible webbing, used in creating fusible appliqué designs.

Stipple quilting: Close background quilting (less than ½" apart) used to create a surface texture and raise the area it surrounds.

Straight grain: Woven threads of the fabric running parallel and perpendicular to the selvage, i.e. the cross-grain and the lengthwise grain.

Strip piecing: Technique in which strips of fabric are cut and joined lengthwise, then counter-cut across the seam lines to form segments. The segments are joined to create units or blocks for the quilt top.

Templates: Shapes made of sturdy material used to trace designs on fabric.

Tied quilt: Quilt in which ties are used to hold the three layers of the quilt together. Technically, these are comforters and not quilts since they have no quilting stitches.

Unfinished size: Size of a strip or fabric piece before it is joined to other pieces of fabric. Also used for blocks and completed quilt tops. The unfinished size includes the seam allowance.

Wrong side: Back or underside of the fabric.

References

Ball, Maggie. *Creative Quilting with Kids*. Iola, WI: Krause Publications, 2001.

Eikmeier, Barbara J. *Kids Can Quilt*. Bothell, WA: That Patchwork Place, 1997.

Fons, Marianne, and Liz Porter. *Quilter's Complete Guide*. Birmingham, AL: Oxmoor House, Inc., and Leisure Arts, Inc., 1993.

McCloskey, Marsha. *Marsha McCloskey's Guide to Rotary Cutting (Revised)*. Seattle, WA: Feathered Star Productions, 1993.

McClun, Diana and Laura Nownes. *Quilts, Quilts, Quilts—The Complete Guide to Quilt Making*. Gualala, CA: The Quilt Digest, 1988.

Noble, Maurine. *Machine Quilting Made Easy!* Bothell, WA: That Patchwork Place, 1994.

Rolfe, Margaret with Beryl Hodges and Judy Turner. *Metric Quiltmaking*. Rozelle, New South Wales: Sally Milner Publishing, 1993.

Viking Sewing Machines Inc. *Sew Young, Sew Fun. Sew It Up!* Westlake, OH: Sewing Information Resources, 2002.

Walters, Cindy. *Snippet Sensations*. Iola, WI: Krause Publications, 1999.

Willing, Karen and Dock, Julie. *Fabric Fun for Kids: Step-by-Step Projects for Children*. Ashland, OR: Now and Then Publications, 1997.

Supply Sources

Sewing Machines
Husqvarna Viking
31000 Viking Parkway
Westlake, OH 44145-8012.
(440) 808-6550
(800) 358-0001

Extension Tables for Sewing Machines
Dream World, Inc.
Paradise Valley/Country Road 21
Bonners Ferry, ID 83805
(208) 267-7136
(800) 837-3261

Quilt Wizard—¼" Seam Allowance Guide
Wizard Attachment Co., Inc.
12999 S. Parker Road, #121
Parker, CO 80134
(866) 994-9273

Fabric
David Textiles, Inc.
1920 S. Tubeway Avenue
City of Commerce, CA 90040
(323) 728-8231
(800) 548-1818

Rotary Cutters, Mats, and Rulers
Prym Dritz Corporation
PO Box 5028
Spartanburg, SC 29304
(864) 587-5265
(800) 845-4948

Thread and Pearl Cotton
Coats & Clark
Consumer Services
PO Box 12229
Greenville, SC 29612-0229
(800) 648-1479

Decorative Threads
Sulky of America, Inc.
3113 Broadpoint Drive
Harbor Heights, FL 33983
(941) 629-3199
(800) 874-4115

Pillow Forms
Fairfield Processing Corporation
88 Rose Hill Avenue
PO Box 1157
Danbury, CT 06813-1157
(203) 980-0989
(800) 744-2090

Batting
The Stearns Technical Textile Company
100 Williams Street
Cincinnati, OH 45215
(513) 948-5252
(800) 345-7150

Steam-a-Seam 2 and Batting
The Warm Co.
954 East Union St.
Seattle, WA 98122
(206) 320-9276
(800) 234-WARM

Fabric Markers, Fantastix, and Stamp Pads
Tsukineko Inc.
17640 NE 65th Street
Redmond, WA 98052
(425) 883-7733

Fabric for Ink-Jet Printing from a Computer
ColorPlus Fabrics, Color Textiles Inc.
9030 West Sahara, #198
Las Vegas, NV 89117
(702) 845-5584

Commercial Machine Quilting
Wanda Rains, Rainy Day Quilts
www.rainydayquilts.com
(360) 297-5115

Carol Latham, Carol's Finishing Touches
(206) 842-0156

PROJECT
PARTICIPANTS

Age in years shown in brackets:

Valerie Olson (15)—Arlington, Washington

Hazel Ball (18), Sophie Lowell (12), Jacqueline (9), and Lisa Schmidt (11)—Bainbridge Island, Washington

Bradford (8) and Harrison Halter (11)—Bothell, Washington

Harry (7), Lily (10), and Holly Hough (11)—London, United Kingdom

Megan Wissler (8)—Kenmore, Washington

Hollie Peterson (15) and Keri Winterhalter (16)—Stanwood, Washington

Hyla Middle School, Bainbridge Island, Washington 6th, 7th and 8th graders (11-14 years):

Zack Acker, Kate Barker, Susie Callahan, Laurel Curran, Griffen Dunn, Shane Elliott, Connor Folse, Miles Freeborn, Karis Hanson, Donna Horning, Katherine Jennings, Laetitia Lehman-Pearsall, Annie Lukins, Alicen Matthews, Layne Matthews, Kira McGieson, Megan Mendenhall, Sarah Powers, Emily Safford, Grace Salisbury, Lucy Schlesser, Emily Schuetz, Ben Skotheim, Megan Smith, Alexandra Tayara, Emelie Van Vleet, and Morgan Wainio.

Hyla Middle School Alumni, Bainbridge Island, Washington:

Katie Allen (15) and Ramona Freeborn (15).

Appendix 1: Block Patterns

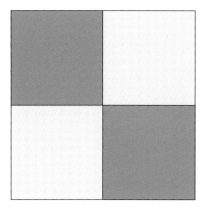

4-Patch: Simple 4-Patch

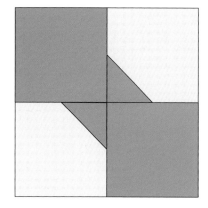

4-Patch: Bowtie

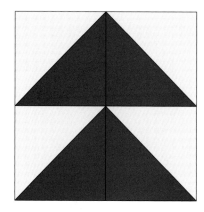

4-Patch: Flying Geese

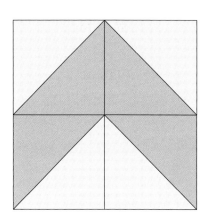

4-Patch: Chevron or
Streak of Lightning

4-Patch: Sawtooth

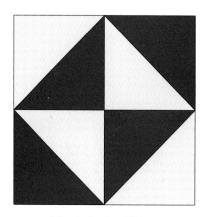

4-Patch: Broken Dishes

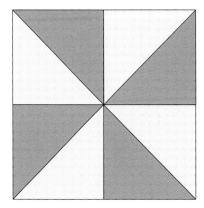

4-Patch: Pinwheel

4-Patch: Double 4-Patch

4-Patch: Double 4-Patch with
Appliqué Hearts

9-Patch: Simple 9-Patch

9-Patch: Shoo Fly

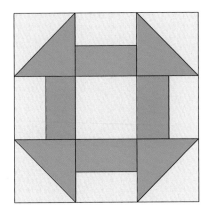

9-Patch: Churn Dash or
Monkey Wrench

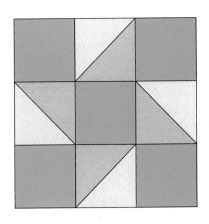

9-Patch: Wings in a Whirl

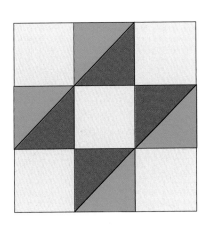

9-Patch: Contrary Wife

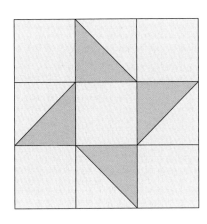

9-Patch: Friendship Star

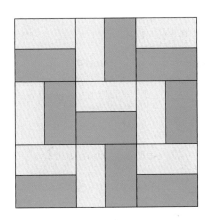

9-Patch: London Stairs

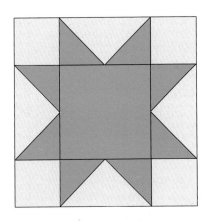

16-Patch: Star

Appliqué Heart

Appendix 2: Cutting for 9" and 12" Quilt Blocks

	9" Blocks	**12" Blocks**
Simple 4-patch	(4) 5" squares (2 light, 2 dark)	(4) 6½" squares (2 light, 2 dark)
Bowtie	(4) 5" squares (2 Bowtie, 2 background) (2) 2½" squares (Bowtie)	(4) 6½" squares (2 Bowtie, 2 background) (2) 3" squares (Bowtie)
Double 4-patch	(2) 5" squares 4 light 2¾" squares, 4 dark 2¾" squares, or strip piece 2 strips (1 light and 1 dark 2¾" x 13" sewn and counter cut (4) 2¾")	(2) 6½" squares 4 light 3½" squares, 4 dark 3½" square, or strip piece 2 strips (1 light and 1 dark 3½" x 16" sewn and counter-cut (4) 3½") Option—add hearts to large squares
Pinwheel, Sawtooth, Broken Dishes, Chevron, Flying Geese, Design your own using Half-square triangles	2 light 5⅜" squares 2 dark 5⅜" squares	2 light 6⅞" squares 2 dark 6⅞" squares
Simple 9-patch	(9) 3½" squares (5 dark and 4 light, or 4 dark and 5 light)	(9) 4½" squares (5 dark and 4 light, or 4 dark and 5 light)
Shoo Fly Friendship Star Contrary Wife Wings in a Whirl Design your own using half-square triangles and squares	(5) 3½" squares (Shoo Fly – 1 dark, 4 light) (Friendship Star – 5 light) (Contrary Wife – 5 light) (Wings in a Whirl – 5 medium) (2) light 3⅞" squares (2) dark 3⅞" squares	(5) 4½" squares (Shoo Fly – 1 dark, 4 light) (Friendship Star – 5 light) (Contrary Wife – 5 light) (Wings in a Whirl – 5 medium) 2 light 4⅞" squares 2 dark 4⅞" squares
Churn Dash or Monkey Wrench	(1) 3½" square 2 light 3⅞" squares 2 dark 3⅞" squares Rectangles – 4 light and 4 dark 3½" x 2", or 2 strips (1 light and 1 dark 2" x 16" sewn and counter-cut (4) 3½")	(1) 4½" square 2 light 4⅞" squares 2 dark 4⅞" squares Rectangles – 4 light and 4 dark 4½" x 2½", or 2 strips (1 light and 1 dark 2½" x 20" sewn and counter-cut (4) 4½")
London Stairs	2 strips (1 light and 1 dark) 2" x 34" sewn and counter-cut (9) 3½"	2 strips (1 light and 1 dark) 2½" x 42" sewn and counter cut (9) 4½"
Star (16-patch)	5" square Background: (4) 2¾" squares, (4) 5" x 2¾" rectangles Star points: (8) 2¾" squares	6½" square Background: (4) 3½" squares, (4) 6½" x 3½" rectangles Star points: (8) 3½" squares

Appendix 3: Heart Templates

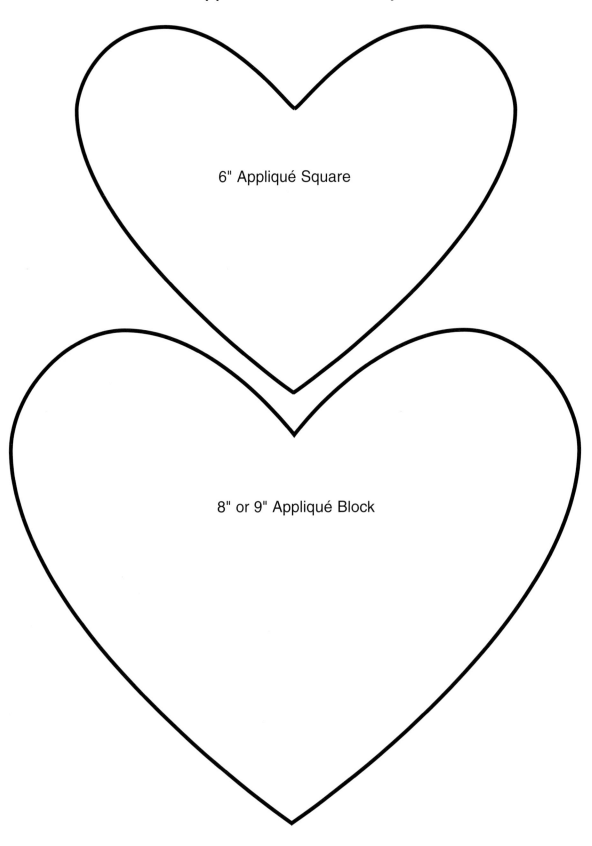

6" Appliqué Square

8" or 9" Appliqué Block

Appendix 4: 4-Patch Grids

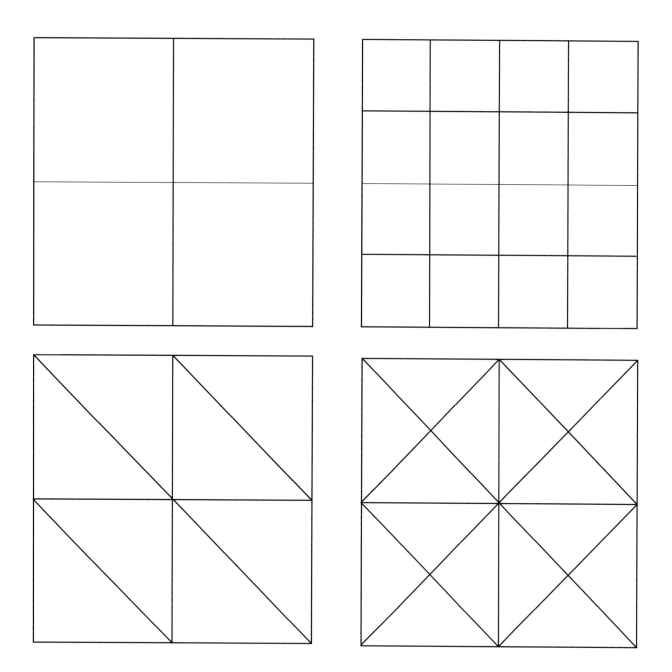

Appendix 5: 9-Patch Grid

Appendix 6: 25-Patch Grid

Appendix 7: Four Bowtie Blocks

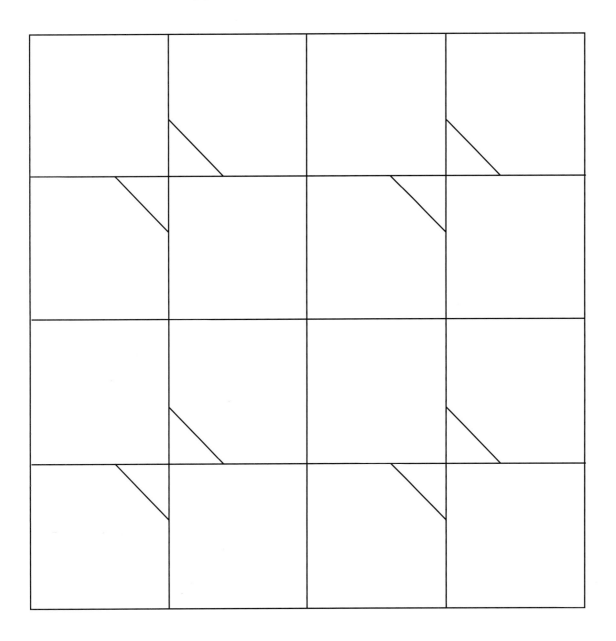

Appendix 8: 16 Half-Square Triangle Units

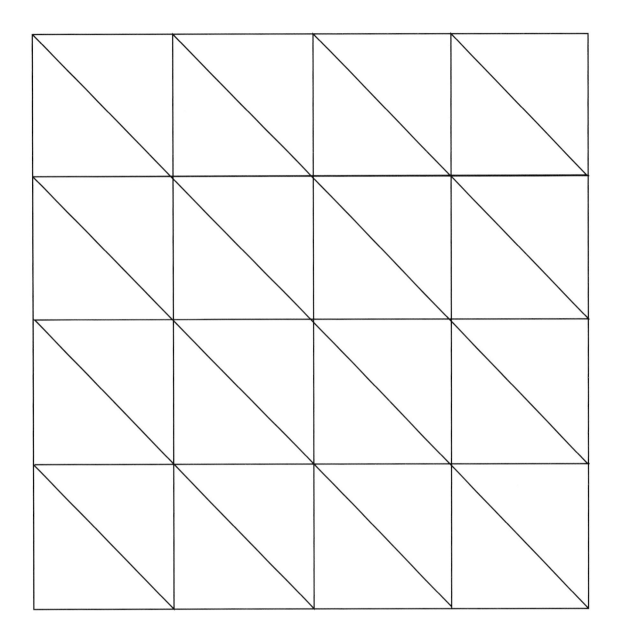

Appendix 9: Ohio Star

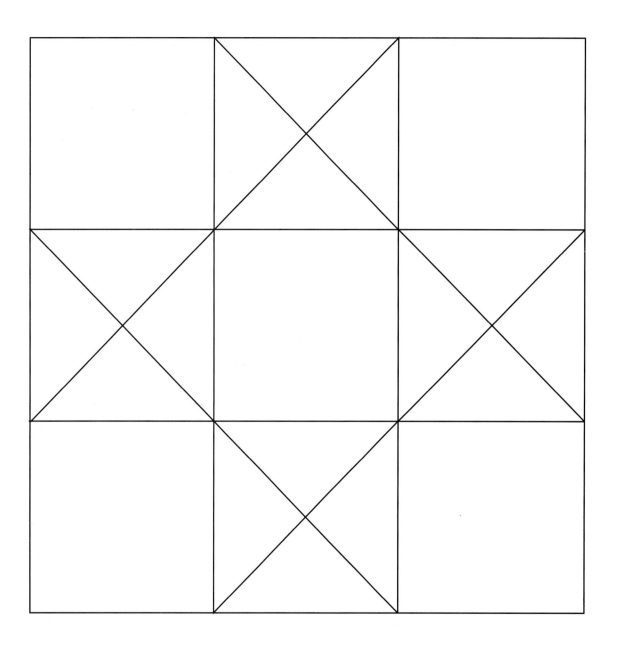

Appendix 10: 81-Patch Grid

Appendix 11: 4-Patch and Squares Grid

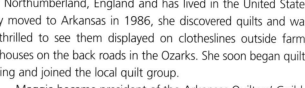

About the Author

Maggie Ball is a native of Northumberland, England and has lived in the United States since 1983. When her family moved to Arkansas in 1986, she discovered quilts and was

thrilled to see them displayed on clotheslines outside farmhouses on the back roads in the Ozarks. She soon began quilting and joined the local quilt group.

Maggie became president of the Arkansas Quilters' Guild in 1992. This group includes several exceptionally talented quilters whose innovative approaches to both traditional and contemporary quilting were inspiring and influential. Here, Maggie organized her first classroom quilt projects with second graders at her children's school.

Since 1993, Maggie, Nigel, and their two children, Hazel and Thomas, have lived on Bainbridge Island near Seattle in the Pacific Northwest. Maggie's quilting projects with over 800 Island children led to the publication of her first book, *Creative Quilting with Kids*, (Krause Publications, 2001). She teaches quilting to all ages, enjoys making art quilts, and has had her award-winning quilts exhibited locally, nationally and internationally. Her work includes a variety of styles and techniques, a small sample of which are displayed here.

Maggie is also a trained judge of quilts and wearable art, certified by the Northern California Quilt Council. Recently she became a consultant with David Textiles, Inc., to help design lines of fabrics for young, and young at heart quilters. A gallery of many of her quilts and further information is available at her Web site: www.DragonflyQuilts.com.

FROM RIGHT CLOCKWISE:
Helios Searches for the Perfect Stem, 44" x 35", designed, hand appliquéd, hand and machine quilted by Maggie Ball, 1996.

Wedding Quilt for Deborah and Joseph, 82" x 82", designed and pieced by Maggie Ball, machine quilted by Wanda Rains, 2001. Commissioned by the congregation of St. Barnabas Church, Bainbridge Island. In the collection of Joseph and Deborah Hickey-Tiernan.

Celestial Garden, 84" x 84", designed and pieced by Maggie Ball, machine quilted by Wanda Rains, 2002.

Soul Mates Dance Forever, 81" x 81", designed and pieced by Maggie Ball, machine quilted by Wanda Rains, 2001. Commission by Jim and Cheryl Hayward for their daughter's wedding. In the collection of Shanna and Josquin Poirot.

CREATE QUILTS FOR ALL AGES

The Essential Guide to Practically Perfect Patchwork
by Michele Morrow Harer

Quilt quickly and easily with the mountain of helpful tips and techniques found in this new book! Beginning with the basics of quilting and then expanding to more advanced concepts, each of the 10 lessons builds on the previous one and allows even the most novice quilter to create fabulous quilts. Both machine and hand quilting are covered.

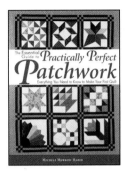

Softcover • 8¼x10⅞ • 160 pages
300+ color photos and illus.
Item# PPPWK • $21.95

Granny Quilts
Vintage Quilts of the '30s Made New for Today
by Darlene Zimmerman

Make a gorgeous quilt, reminiscent of the 1930s, with the help of this creative new book. You'll explore the history and style of the '30s quilts, while learning to replicate them with reproduction fabrics and 19 beautiful projects. A variety of appliquéd and pieced quilts are featured

Softcover • 8¼x10⅞ • 128 pages
150+ color photos & illus.
Item# GRANQ • $21.95

Creative Quilting with Kids
by Maggie Ball

Kids love to create. In this book parents, teachers and group leaders will find more than 40 exciting projects to keep them both happy and busy. Children ages 5-15 learn to create beautiful quilts appropriate to their skill level, using techniques from hand quilting to machine quilting. If you love quilting and working with children, you will treasure these projects and the countless hours of joy they will bring.

Softcover • 8¼x10⅞ • 144 pages
200 color photos
Item# CQUIL • $24.95

Colorful Quilts for Kids
by Beth Wheeler

Wrap your child in love with a quilt you made especially for him or her. Using the detailed instructions and illustrations, you'll learn how to make 20 cute and comforting quilts with motifs that are inspired by whimsical embroidery designs of the '30s, '40s, and '50s.

Softcover • 8¼x10⅞
• 128 pages
100 color photos & 25 illus.
Item# BABYQ • $21.95

Fast Patch® Kids' Quilts
Dozens of Designs To Make for and with Kids
by Anita Hallock and Betsy Hallock Heath

The unique Fast Patch® technique allows you to create checkerboards and tricky triangles from simple sewn strips. Kids will love the 20 different quilt blocks featuring birds, fish, butterflies and clowns. Margin symbols tell you when kids can help too!

Softcover • 8¼x10⅞ • 112 pages
color section
Item# FPKQ • $22.95

Raw Edge Appliqué
by Jodie Davis

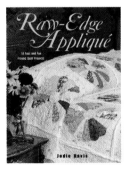

Imagine making a Dresden Plate minus fussy needle-turn appliqué or an Orange Peel without matching a curve ... with Jodie Davis' new book, you can! You'll find 10 fun and fast quilt projects that eliminate hours of pinning and matching by using a straight machine stitch. The raw edges are left exposed to become slightly frayed as the quilt is loved, laundered—and loved some more.

Softcover • 8¼x10⅞ • 96 pages
20 color photos
Item# FEQ • $19.95